THE REFORM OF THE CHRISTIAN CHURCH

by
Henry C. Smith

A Hearthstone Book

Carlton Press, Inc.　　　　　　　New York, N.Y.

Scripture text (unless otherwise noted): Holy Bible, New International Version, copyright © 1978, New York Bible Society. Used by permission.

© 1983 by Henry C. Smith
ALL RIGHTS RESERVED
Manufactured in the United States of America
ISBN 0-8062-1987-4

Acknowledgment

I wish to thank the following people in particular for their suggestions, encouragement, and help in the preparation of this work: Donald E. Nalls, Jr., J. Robert Sowers, Joyce K. Smith, and Robin Bennett.

Table of Contents

Introduction

Chapter 1   The Basis of Reform: The Authority of God   11

Chapter 2   The Goal of Reform: Submission to the Authority of God   19

Chapter 3   The First Condition of Reform: Coping with the Unregenerate Influence in the Church—Part I   27

Chapter 4   Coping with the Unregenerate Influence in the Church—Part II: Practical Considerations..   45

Chapter 5   The Second Condition of Reform: God's Authority in the Christian Life   57

Chapter 6   The Third Condition of Reform: God's Authority in the Collective Church   65

Chapter 7   Conclusions   87

Footnotes   95

Introduction

The purpose of this book is not to present a study of previous reform movements that have taken place within the Christian Church, but rather, to map out a logical course by which the godly reader might work towards a reformation in this present age. Throughout its extensive history, there have been numerous times when the church fell into a state of degeneration, and required a subsequent reformation period in which to rebuild. Judging from the number of new denominations which have been formed in recent years, along with the fact that the majority of them seem to place some emphasis on returning to what might be called "traditional" beliefs, it would appear that many persons are dissatisfied with the condition of some churches as they presently stand, and feel that the time has once again come for reform. This is further substantiated by the fact that the (generally) smaller, more conservative churches seem to be showing a growth at this time, whereas the larger, more liberal denominations are, almost as a rule, losing members or showing little growth. The extent to which a reform is actually needed, or whether it is needed at all, might be considered debatable in some circles; but when we look about us and see churches giving financial aid to terrorists,[1] throwing their support behind homosexual groups,[2] and encouraging such things as abortion and fornication,[3] surely no one will argue that there is no room left for improvement. This book has therefore been written to help the reader understand just which forces in the church are degenerative in nature, and to set forth methods by which they may be eliminated.

Probably the most common mistake modern reformers have been guilty of is to concentrate on the "effects" of evil, without going to the source of the problem. We could say, for instance, that the present-day tolerance of abortion in some churches is an evil, but even if this manifestation was actually removed, little progress would have been made, for the degenerative forces which originally caused this effect are still there, waiting for another chance to rear their heads. It is not enough to merely beat down the effects of evil; a successful reform movement must be able to cope with the origin of the problems. Therefore, a systematic approach must be taken—an approach which will get to the very heart of the church's problems and deal adequately with the causes of degeneration, without becoming sidetracked on crusades to stamp out only the effects of such forces.

In order to do this, and to outline a plan of action, we must think seriously about such questions as these: "From what source or sources do degenerative tendencies come? By what means does sin enter the church? What exactly is a sinful or degenerative force? What is a regenerative force? On what basis can we define these terms? Once we have a means of defining them, how do we deal with them?" These are the questions we must confront in any serious reform movement.

In this book, I have sought to deal with these questions in such a way as to present to the reader a logical and orderly summary of these points. Lest we be accused of superficiality, let the reader understand that a topic of this magnitude can be treated only summarily in a work of this size. Our purpose here is not to lay out an inflexible plan which encompasses every detail, but to present an outline of thought which may be adapted to a variety of situations. Neither do we make any extravagant claims that the publication of this book will result in a reformation; for writing a book, and motivating people to follow it, are clearly two entirely different things. My only claim concerning this system is that if we examine any given problem within the church closely enough, we will find its existence there to be a derivative of the matters discussed here.

Clearly, reform is a continual process, and it is the responsibility of each generation of Christians to attempt to correct any existing detrimental beliefs or customs. The fact that God has sovereign control over these matters, and that true reform comes only rarely, does not excuse us in the least; for it is always the duty of every Christian to strive for the purity and holiness of His church. Let us, therefore, apply ourselves to this task, so that we need not be ashamed on the Day of Reckoning for having neglected our responsibilities.

THE REFORM OF THE CHRISTIAN CHURCH

Chapter 1

The Basis of Reform: The Authority of God

Any system of church reform must be built upon an authoritative foundation. By definition, "reform" indicates an improvement or correction; but without an authoritative standard which will define these terms with respect to the church, the precise meaning of "improvement" or "correction" is largely subjective and dependent upon the judgment of the individual. Hence, "improvement" from the standpoint of one person could be judged as retrogression from the standpoint of another, with no manner of determining which one, if either, is correct. When this situation exists, the meaning of "reform" is susceptible to as many interpretations as there are reformers.

Such a subjective approach to the topic of reform would clearly be a waste of time. For if there is no means of determining whose concept of reform is the correct one, then there is no means of knowing when reform has been achieved, or if any progress has been made. Right and wrong, good and evil, reformed and unreformed, all become hazy terms definable only on a relativistic basis. Authentic reform can be defined only when these terms are fixed by an authority external to ourselves.

From the viewpoint of the Christian religion, the only sound basis for a system of reform is the authority of God. Because God is the Creator and Owner of the universe, He is the absolute ruler and final authority on all matters—the church is His to do with as He pleases. Only He has the authority to determine what its purpose is, or state what will constitute perfection in it.

There is no other being who can rightfully lay a claim to this position of authority. Certainly no mere man can take this privilege upon himself, and use his own reasoning as a basis for the reformation of God's church. For the church belongs to God; it is not man's to trifle with. When we visit someone's home, for instance, it is automatically assumed that the owner is to be the final authority regarding the rules of that house. The person who barges into another man's home and attempts to enforce his own standards upon that man's family is considered arrogant, indeed. Similarly, the standards of perfection and reform within the church cannot be set by just anyone. Only God, the owner, has that privilege.

Furthermore, the true Christian is logically compelled to acknowledge that God possesses this authority. Since the church is by definition composed of those who follow Christ, then it is clear that anyone who rejects Christ's authority and will not follow Him is not a true member of His church. So, while there are some who will not accept God as the ultimate authority in this matter, those who call themselves "Christian" are bound to do so, lest they betray a serious inconsistency.

With the authority of God recognized as the basis of reform, we now have a means of defining regenerative and degenerative tendencies in the Christian Church. Throughout the remainder of this work, reform will be defined as "any thought, action, or communication which enforces or encourages obedience to God (through lawful means)." A degenerative tendency will be defined as "any thought, action, or communication which enforces or encourages disobedience to God's revealed decrees, or in any way works to supplant God's authority with any other." From this it follows that our goal in reform is to encourage obedience to, and acceptance of, God's authority within all members of the church. For it is upon God's authority alone that we can base the church's standards, purposes, and goals.

Reform Must be Based on the Scriptures

This being the case, the next point to be considered is the method by which God makes known His will for the church. It would be of little value to know that God's authority is the sole basis for reformation, if there is no means of discovering the terms of that rule.

The most authoritative source we have concerning the things

of God is the Bible. Historically, the Scriptures have been the common authority of Christendom, and in all matters of controversy between Christians they are accepted as the highest court of appeal. Inspired by God, they put forth in a lasting form the revelation of God to men, that there be no mistake concerning the plan of God for the church and the way of salvation. And while it is true that God reveals Himself to us in other ways, the Bible is the only means He has given by which this revelation can be interpreted both reliably and objectively. The Bible is therefore our primary guide not only in the Christian life, but in reform of the church as well.

It is clear that only the Bible can serve in this role. The Christian Church cannot rely on any other source to speak authoritatively on the things of God, because only this book claims inspiration and can substantiate that assertion. No person, acting merely on his own observations and judgments, can discover from natural sources the basis principles of reform; any revelation concerning these matters must be sent by God Himself, written in a finished and comprehensive character that man's mind can grasp. Therefore, a reliable revelation carrying God's authority must be independent of and objective to man. The Bible is the only standard we have of this description; our own interpretation of other forms of revelation must by necessity be largely or wholly subjective, and hence, unreliable. Thus, the Scriptures must serve as the final authority by which any system of reform is judged.

In one sense, the acceptance of God's Word is a subjective experience, of course. As Christians, the final and strongest confirmation regarding this matter is the working of the Holy Spirit in our hearts, that we come to accept God's Word and learn to love it. The Holy Spirit enlightens the true believer's mind and causes him to love God and want to obey His every decree. But the Spirit is merely confirming in our hearts what the Scriptures already say; the Spirit cannot and will not instruct us to violate or disregard the law of God. Hence, even in this subjective form of assurance, God is using it solely for the purpose of confirming what has already been revealed objectively.

It would, of course, be misleading to claim that no one disputes these statements. The vast hordes of men who attack the authority of the Bible supply abundant proof that many do not hold it in such esteem. Christians should not be surprised at this, though, for the unsaved man must reject the Scriptures in order to maintain a degree of consistency in his life. Indeed, if he is to justify his sinful lifestyle, this is a necessity. From the unsaved man the church can expect nothing else.

But from the standpoint of church reformation, the major problem is not that unsaved men reject the Scriptures. The opinions of men on the outside who are totally unconcerned about the affairs of the church rarely cause that much trouble. The problem is that there are many who consider themselves Christians and still hold to this view. This is what we must beware of. For to think that one belongs to God when he has no respect for His Word is inconsistent, to say the least. When it progresses to the point of arrogance where he can dogmatically reject God's Word as the basis of church structure, this view is no longer just inconsistent—it is Satanic.

It is not difficult to expose the folly of such men. For in their zeal to usurp the authority of the Bible, they can never deny themselves the pleasure of taking God's place. No matter how they approach this situation, they cannot succeed in destroying the authority of the Scriptures without substituting subjective judgments of their own, and making man the final point of reference. It matters not whether we are discussing a simple system, or any number of more elaborate systems thought up by critical theologians in recent years—they all must suffer from this one inherent defect at some point. For how can they even challenge the authority of God's Word, without starting on the assumption that they themselves are qualified to sit in judgment on the infinite? When they so pompously state that certain portions of the Scriptures no longer need apply, are they not in actuality stating that they need not apply—in their opinion? Even when they attempt to refute the Bible by purely scientific or historical means, that is, in an objective manner, they must start out on the assumption that they themselves possess full and absolute knowledge of these matters; otherwise, later findings may force them to change their judgments. Neither can they account for the possibility of supernatural intervention. Hence, man does not possess the capability of refuting the Bible objectively. Any attempts to prove the Bible wrong must start on the assumption that man's reason is the ultimate authority.

This, of course, automatically destroys their case. For whether man tries to make himself the ultimate authority from the beginning, or piously asserts that God is the ultimate authority and then rejects the parts of His revelation which doesn't please him, the results are the same: an unstable church founded solely on the whims of man. But we already know that true reform can be based only on the authority of God. Hence, attempting to reform the church when God's authoritative revelation is not considered trustworthy is just as hopeless as if we had no objective authority at all. Regardless of how long and diligently we toy with such a system, there is no means of ever reaching any definite conclusions (other than that such a system is worthless).

In his *Institutes of the Christian Religion*, John Calvin, probably the greatest theologian since the Apostle Paul, lashes out at those who would make the Scriptures subservient to the judgment of men:

> But a most pernicious error widely prevails that Scripture has only so much weight as is conceded to it by the consent of the church. As if the eternal and inviolable truth of God depended upon the decision of men! For they mock the Holy Spirit when they ask: Who can convince us that these writings came from God? Who can assure us that Scripture has come down whole and intact to our very day? Who can persuade us to receive one book in reverence but to exclude another, unless the church prescribe a sure rule for all these matters? What reverence is due Scripture and what books ought to be reckoned within its canon depend, they say, upon the determination of the church. Thus, these sacrilegious men, wishing to impose an unbridled tyranny under the cover of the church, do not care with what absurdities they ensnare themselves and others, provided they can force this one idea upon the simple-minded: that the church has authority in all things. Yet, if this is so, what will happen to miserable consciences seeking firm assurance of eternal life if all promises of it consist in and depend solely upon the judgment of men? Will they cease to vacillate and tremble when they receive such an answer? Again, to what mockeries of the impious is our faith subjected, into what suspicion has it fallen among all men, if we believe that it has a precarious authority dependent solely upon the good pleasure of men!
> (*Institutes*, Book I, VII, 1).[1]

Despite the fact that Calvin intended this primarily as a refutation to the Roman Church of his century, does it not apply equally in our day to those who seek to remove God's Word as the authoritative base of the church?

As Christians, we must remember that Jesus regarded the Scriptures as totally authoritative. There can be no doubt that He regarded them as our rule of life. When confronted by adversaries, His means of silencing them was to reply, "It is written...." After quoting the Scripture, that settled the matter. (While this refers only to the Old Testament, the New Testament books likewise have been accepted as canonical only on the same grounds as the Old.)

Those who are to be His followers, then, are compelled to do the same. If Jesus believed the Scriptures to be authoritative and unbreakable (John 10:35), then no one can call himself a follower of Christ and refuse to do so. "A student is not above his teacher, but everyone who is fully trained will be like his teacher" (Luke 6:40) (NIV). Jesus constantly lived a life of holiness, always mindful of the Word of God. The Christian is therefore expected to pursue the same course as his Master, and that course includes Jesus' dedication to the Scriptures as the sole authority for our lives.

Those who reject the authority of Scripture then, likewise reject the leadership of Christ. As a result, they have no just grounds for applying the term "Christian" to themselves, nor do they rightfully belong in the Christian Church. To claim that they cannot trust the Scriptures, and yet believe that Christ died for them, is utter nonsense. For once they reject the authority of Scripture, they have no solid basis left on which to believe that Jesus even existed.

The true Christian cannot forget that an all-wise and all-powerful God is in control of this universe—a God who is capable of maintaining His own book in any form He chooses. To deliberately allow errors of any magnitude to maintain themselves in His manuscript, and hence allow a perverted revelation to modify the beliefs and actions of His chosen people, is totally out of line with the character of the Christian God. To even suggest that He would do so is blasphemy.

The true Christian is therefore bound to accept the Scriptures as his rule of life. As his Master does, so does he. He does not recoil from this, but rejoices in it; for to all who are of God, His

Spirit comes upon them and makes them of like mind to the end that they might be holy (Eph. 1:4). The true Christian does not seek to overthrow the authority of Scripture, nor does he want to.

In order to achieve any degree of holiness within the church, either individually or collectively, we must begin by looking to God for guidance. Only God can correctly define what is right and wrong, good and evil, holy and unholy. Only He can establish the standards of perfection for either the Christian life or the collective church. Any attempt by man to seize this authority for himself is not only wrong, since the church does not belong to him, but likewise is doomed to failure simply because such a path can only lead into a confused nightmare of relativism. Any true system of church reform must, by necessity, follow the example of Christ our Lord, and submit itself to the authority of God, as revealed to us in the Scriptures.

Chapter 2

The Goal of Reform: Submission to the Authority of God

Once we acknowledge the Scriptures to be the final authority by which a system is to be judged, the process of reform becomes primarily a matter of enforcing obedience to that standard. For of what value would it be to specify an authority on which to base a reformation, if there is no intention of conforming to it? To acknowledge that God is the Supreme Authority of the universe is of little benefit if recognition of that fact does not result in due submission.

Therefore, the objective of any true reform movement must be not only to acknowledge the authority of Scripture, but to actually bring the church into a state of submission to this standard. And while the church on earth cannot attain unto perfection, composed as it is of fallible humans, the fact remains that progress is possible, as can be demonstrated from the numerous times in which the church fell into error and was later brought into periods of revival. This progress, however, can only be measured with respect to the Scriptures—for the meaning of the term "progress," with respect to any movement, is inherently defined by the authority on which the system is built. Hence, the true Christian Church, which acknowledges only the Bible as its objective authority, can truly claim to be in a state of reform or revival only when all factors are producing a trend towards greater submission to God's Word. Similarly, any trends within the church which lead away from strict obedience to God's Word are disruptive and degenerative. These degenerative tendencies may even include programs which might appear good in themselves, but which tend to nevertheless take the church's emphasis off of God—such as undue emphasis on social programs, and other such things which might be motivated by humanistic thought. The church is truly in a state of reform only when it is in the process of returning to a state of submission to God's Word.

It is important that we fully recognize this fact, for much of the present confusion in the churches is due to a misunderstanding of the church's purpose. The Christian must always remember that his sole purpose of existence, and of the church collectively, is to know God and to glorify Him through obedience and submission to His will. In Ecclesiastes 12:13, the Preacher tells us that to reverence God and obey His commandments is the whole duty of man. The Apostle Paul tells us that everything man does is to be done for God's glory (I Cor. 10:31). And in John 14, Christ Himself emphasizes the fact that those who will not obey Him are not truly right with Him (vs. 23, 24). Throughout the Bible, man is repeatedly shown that he was given life solely for the purpose of having communion with God, and that he must submit his will to the Lord if he is to live.

The reason man is required to submit his will to God is clear: As the Creator of the universe, God is the Owner of all things, and all of His creatures are therefore bound to submit to His decrees. We are not our own, we are the Lord's; He has created us solely for His own purposes. And if God's purpose in the creation of man is solely to bring glory to Himself, then man has no purpose of existence other than this. Hence, any attempt by man to overthrow or rebel against the authority of God automatically destroys any justification for man's existence. He becomes like a pen with no ink, or a drinking glass with a hole in the bottom. Although he exists, he is worthless for the one purpose for which he was created.

Obedience, then, not only pleases God, but in reality justifies man's very existence; and what holds for the individual in this case likewise holds for the church as a whole. Obedience is not only desirable from God's church, but in a very real sense is a necessity; this is why all true members of the church will someday stand fully sanctified in God's presence. For a disobedient church would be, so far as God's purpose of creation goes, worthless.

Thus, in any true system of reform, the church must be willing to do more than acknowledge the authority of Scripture—it must also submit to it and obey. For man is not justified by merely acknowledging the existence and authority of God, or even that the Scriptures are man's rule of life. For as the Scriptures themselves point out, even the demons believe in God and know about Him (James 2:19); what makes them evil is that they have no desire to do what He says. Likewise, a mere intellectual assent by man is not enough, for all such thinking is nothing more than a mental exercise if it does not produce in us a desire to obey.

Man's Response to the Authority of God

The Scriptures teach clearly that strict obedience to God is the duty of all men, but this fact should not be allowed to lead us to hasty and unrealistic conclusions concerning the true state of man. For these same Scriptures which so clearly proclaim God's law and the proper response which man should render also reveal to us the fact that man is a sinner—a being in a state of rebellion against God. The Bible tells us that everyone has turned away, and that none are truly righteous in God's sight (Romans 3:10).

Man fell into this state when Adam, acting as the federal head of the human race, chose to disobey God and placed his own judgment ahead of the Lord's. This sin, like all sin which has subsequently followed, was an open rebellion against the authority of God, and hence, severed man's close relationship with Him. The sinful nature which causes this alienation from God has been passed on to all of Adam's descendants; so all men, in their natural state, are essentially at enmity with God, lost in their sins, and totally unable to help themselves out of their depraved condition (Eph.2).

The central question which the church must come to terms with, then, is this: How can man overcome this sinful nature and be restored to a state of holiness before God? Man can only be pleasing unto God when he is in obedience to Him, whether as an individual or as the collective church. In reform, therefore, the goal must be to bring both the individual and the whole into a state of submission to God. But how is this done?

The Bible, the only true authority which can speak on these things, reveals that man in his natural state cannot do anything to become holy through any power of his own. The Scriptures tell us that man can only be pleasing unto God by undergoing a complete change in nature. But even common sense tells us that if a man is so fallen as to be in rebellion against the Lord, then he must undergo a change in nature before he can have any desire to achieve holiness. This point can perhaps be grasped even more easily by thinking in terms of the devil. It is easy enough for us to see that Satan and the demons would have to be given a totally different nature if they were ever to be saved; and yet, in his fallen state, the innate sinful principles which actuate man are of the same nature as those which stimulate fallen angels, even though they may not be revealed quite so intensely in this life. If a man is dead in sin, then nothing short of a supernatural change by the Holy Spirit will ever cause him to do what is spiritually good (John 3:3, Jer. 13:23, I Cor. 2:14, II Cor. 5:17).

In the process of salvation, the converted Christian undergoes just such a change, which is called "regeneration" (Titus 3:5), referred to also by such terms as a new birth (John 3:3), a passing out of death into life (John 5:24), a calling out of darkness into God's marvelous light (I Peter 2:9), and a making alive (Col. 2:13). Regeneration is basically a spiritual resurrection brought about by the same mighty power which God wrought in Christ when He raised him from the dead. It is a sovereign gift of God, graciously bestowed on those whom God has chosen to save, and is totally independent of the will of man.

Regeneration involves an essential change in character. It is making the tree good in order that the fruit might be good. As a result of this change, the person passes from a state of unbelief to one of saving faith. The truly converted Christian comes to see his inability and knows that he does not make himself eligible for heaven by his own good works and merits. Thus, the elect hear the Gospel and believe—not always at the first hearing, but at the divinely appointed time—the non-elect hear but disbelieve, not because they lack sufficient evidence, but because their inward nature is opposed to holiness. The reason for the two kinds of response can only be traced to an external source: "I will give you a new heart and put a new spirit in you; I will remove from you your heart of stone and give you a heart of flesh." (Ezek. 36:26) (NIV).

When a man receives this inward, purifying change of nature, the most immediate and important effect is that he comes to trust in Christ for his salvation, and comes to love righteousness, whereas his old natural element was sin. Sin no longer has total control over him, and he loves to do that which is good. This process of regeneration totally changes a man's outlook on life, as well as converting his will. The Spirit removes the appetite for sinful things so that he refrains from them, and the holy and thorough submission to God's will, which the convert before dreaded and resisted, he now loves and approves.

But while regeneration gives a person saving faith in Christ for salvation, and reorients the will to make the sinner capable of good, it does not render him immediately perfect. As long as people remain in this world they are subject to temptations and they still have the remnants of the old nature clinging to them. Thus, regeneration does not truly make the person perfectly righteous, but gives them the ability to become such.

Sanctification, on the other hand, is the process whereby the remains of sin in the outward life are gradually removed. It consists of the gradual triumph of the new nature implanted in regeneration over the evil that still remains after the heart has been renewed. Perfect righteousness is the goal which is set before us all through this life and every Christian should make steady progress toward that goal. Sanctification, however, is not fully completed until death, at which time the Holy Spirit cleanses the soul of every vestige of sin, making it holy and raising it above even the possibility of sinning. Thus, in reality, complete sanctification lags behind after the life has, in principle, been won to God.[1]

Considering that these processes are for all practical purposes under the control of God, and that it is He who chooses upon whom He will bestow these gifts, it might seem at first to be pointless to even attempt reform. For if the individuals which compose the church can only be brought into a state of holiness by God, then it is clear that only God can produce a state of reform within the church. It would therefore seem logical to conclude that reform is a process beyond the control of man.

This statement is, of course, true. Only God can produce a changed heart. Only God can cause a revival and reform within the church. Any attempt by man to reform the church by his own power must of course end in a most dismal failure.

But on the other hand, it is also true that God often uses human agents by which to accomplish His desired ends. It is true that only God can change a man's heart and save him; but God has chosen, generally, to spread the faith through the preaching of the Gospel, using human agents. Likewise, sanctification is a process by which God works in our hearts; and yet, the Scriptures are full of exhortations to discipline ourselves, and to help in the edification of our fellow Christians. This is not inconsistent, for in the natural realm God works in this same way. Our food, for instance, is given to us totally by God. But if we are to expect a harvest, God makes us work for it. We must plant the crops, fertilize the crops, and water the crops if we are to have any. But God is the One who makes them grow. In a similar fashion, church reformation can be achieved only as God is working in it. But we must expect to work to accomplish it; not that it is brought about by our efforts, but because God has chosen to work in this manner.

It is entirely possible, of course, that God has not ordained that a reformation will take place at this time. But that does not excuse us from working towards that goal. Whether God has decreed that a reformation shall come or not, it is always the Christian's duty to strive for purity in His church, that God's bride be not defiled and profaned by worthless men.

In summary, we find that at least these two factors play a key role in the reclamation of the individual from a sinful nature:

(1) Regeneration—the process through which God gives the man a new nature; and
(2) Sanctification—whereby God works with the person in overcoming the remnant of the sinful nature, whether "directly," when God teaches the individual a point without the aid of human agents, or "indirectly," when He may use other Christians to encourage, direct, or perhaps rebuke as necessary as an aid in their Christian growth.

These factors are indispensable to the growth of the Christian.

In a similar fashion, the church's purity is keyed to these same factors. Just as the individual must undergo these processes to render proper submission to the authority of God, the visible church likewise approaches perfection only as those which compose her partake of these factors. Thus, the entire visible church may not be regenerated, but the greater the number of members who are, the closer the church comes to proper submission. Not everyone in the visible church is truly grappling to overcome the sin which still possesses them as strongly as they should; but the more this is done, the stronger the church becomes. And few people today truly seek to help with the discipline and edification of a Christian brother; but the more we concentrate on these matters, the closer the church comes to a state of perfection.

Since reform of the church involves primarily a collective submission to the authority of God, which can be obtained only through what has just been outlined, the remainder of our study will be an elaboration of these three factors. And while the problems of the church may be complex, they all stem from sources which are basic. In order to understand the process of reform, we need only remember that the church's purpose is to know and glorify God, that man has turned away from this duty in rebellion, and that he can only be restored by first undergoing regeneration, and then progressing through sanctification. With these simple facts in mind, we are now ready to begin the process of reform.

Chapter 3

The First Condition of Reform: Coping with the Unregenerate Influence in the Church

Part 1

In any attempt to return a church to a state of obedience to God, the first point which must be investigated is the distinction between the saved and the unsaved elements which might exist in the membership. For while all men are required to obey God, and all have likewise fallen short, the Scriptures teach that there is a fundamental difference between the nature of the saved man and his unregenerate counterpart. One of the most basic of these dissimilarities is the partial restoration of man's ability to do works pleasing to God through the death of Christ. The Bible tells us that the ability to do works righteous in God's sight has to some extent been restored in salvation, whereas the natural man, still in a state of rebellion against God, is incapable of pleasing Him even with works which would otherwise be good in themselves. Thus, it is clear at the outset that the unregenerate man is not capable of the one thing required in reform: obedience with a right heart. His presence in the church membership can therefore result only in a degenerative effect.

That these statements are true can readily be verified from Scripture. The Bible from beginning to end declares that man in his natural state is fallen and in rebellion against God. (Gen. 3, Romans 5:12-21, I Cor. 15:22, I Tim. 2:13, 14). Man fell into this state when Adam, acting as the federal head of the human race, chose to reject the authority of God and placed his own judgement first (Romans 5:12). Paul demonstrates, in Romans 5:13 and 14, that all men fell with Adam by pointing out the fact that men still died between the time of Adam and Moses, even though they had no specific commandment to break as Adam did. Paul thus concludes that since death is the penalty for sin, all men must possess the same rebellious nature as Adam.

But in Romans 5:15-21, Paul reveals that even this was an act of mercy on God's part. For if men were to be judged solely on their own merits, all would be lost; but since this rebellious nature entered through the actions of one man, then God is just in pardoning those who follow Christ, who serves as the Head of the covenant of grace. Just as sin entered through the disobedience of one man, righteousness can enter through the obedience of one man, Christ Jesus (Romans 5:19), the only man who lived a sinless life. Thus, those whom God chooses to save are made righteous in His sight by the blood of Christ (Romans 5:9), but all those whom God leaves in the natural state are dead in their sins and are in rebellion against Him (Romans 3:10-18, Eph. 2:1-3, I Corin. 1:18, I Corin. 2:14).

It must be emphasized at this point that so long as a man remains in this state of rebellion against the Lord, he is unable to render unto Him the proper obedience which He requires. It is true, of course, that many unsaved people do possess admirable qualities and do perform virtuous acts, when judged by man's standards. But from the spiritual perspective, when judged by God's standards, the unsaved sinner is not capable of good. The unsubmissive and disobedient man's best works are nothing more than "filthy rags" in the sight of God (Isaiah 64:6).

Man naturally tends to think in terms not quite so absolute. He prefers to think rather that all men have a certain degree of goodness about them, the amount merely varying from individual to individual and depending largely on external influences, such as the environment, education, etc. But what he fails to consider is that since man's sole purpose of existence is to live in obedience to God, then anything done for any other reason is worthless in God's sight, regardless of any outward benefits which might result from it.

Hence, while the natural man may perform works which are good in themselves, he cannot do anything of any real merit. So long as he is in a state of rebellion against God, his works all lack the one thing which can truly make them righteous—a love for God. A moral act must always be judged by the standard of love towards God, for a righteous act in God's sight requires a right heart as well as the proper outward motions. (See Acts 5:1-11)

This principle has been very plainly illustrated in an example by W. D. Smith:

In a gang of pirates we may find many things that are good in themselves. Though they are in wicked rebellion against the laws of the government, they have their own laws and regulations, which they obey strictly. We find among them courage and fidelity, with many other things that will recommend them as pirates. They may do many things, too, which the laws of the government require, but they are not done because the government has so required, but in obedience to their own regulations. For instance, the government requires honesty and they may be strictly honest, one with another, in their transactions, and the division of all their spoil. Yet, as respects the government, and the general principle, their whole life is one of the most wicked dishonesty. Now, it is plain, that while they continue in their rebellion they can do nothing to recommend them to the government as citizens. Their first step must be to give up their rebellion, acknowledge their allegiance to the government, and sue for mercy. So all men, in their natural state, are rebels against God, and though they may do many things which the law of God requires, and which will recommend them as men, yet nothing is done with reference to God and His law. Instead, the regulations of society, respect for public opinion, self-interest, their own character in the sight of the world, or some other worldly or wicked motive, reigns supremely, and God, to whom they owe their heart and lives, is forgotten; or, if thought of at all, His claims are wickedly rejected, His counsels spurned, and the heart, in obstinate rebellion, refuses obedience.

"The good actions of unregenerate men," Smith continues, are not positively sinful in themselves, but sinful from defect. They lack the principle which alone can make them righteous in the sight of God. In the case of the pirates it is easy to see that all their actions are sin against the government. While they continue pirates, their sailing, mending, or rigging the vessel, and even their eating and drinking, are all sins in the eyes of the government, as they are only so many expedients to enable them to continue their piratical career, and are parts of their life of rebellion. So with sinners. While the heart is wrong, it vitiates everything in the sight of God, even their most ordinary occupations; for the plain, unequivocal language of God is, "Even the lamp of the wicked, is sin," Prov. 21:4.[1]

Thus we see that the unsaved man cannot in any way please God. God expects obedience; indeed, He demands it, as our Creator. But the natural man will not, by his own choice, even attempt to obey God for any legitimate reason. This fact is confirmed not only by testimony and experience, but also by Scripture itself.

Thus, in conclusion, we find that:

(1) Perfection in the church can only be approached as man's will is surrendered to God in obedience, and
(2) Man in his unsaved state will not, indeed, cannot render to God that obedience which He requires, at least in any form worthy of Him.

It is important that we understand these two points, for all clear thinking on the problems within the church must start here.

The Effect Produced in the Church by the "Unregenerate Christian," and the Biblical Response

Since the proper operation of the church is largely dependent upon obedience to and a respect for God's authority, then it is clear that only the truly saved Christian can contribute to the welfare of the church. Only the true Christian can honestly hate sin and want to repent of it, and only the true Christian honestly wants to please God and submit to His decrees. Because the unsaved man is still in a state of rebellion, he can never do anything of any real merit, regardless of any outward display he may generate. He desires first of all to please himself and to assert his own authority, and thereby places himself in direct opposition to God, as do all who restlessly clamor for their "rights." He is therefore incapable of true submission to the Lord.

Because the Christian's view of life is totally God-centered, and the unsaved man's view is self-centered, it is obvious that their opinions concerning many things must be in radical opposition. One group, under the influence of the Holy Spirit, seeks to do the will of God, and learns to submit to His authority, and to those authorities which God has placed over them. The other group, under the power of Satan, seeks to follow their own self-centered desires. The unsaved man is guided by a totally different set of basic principles than is his Christian counterpart.

Living together on the same planet, however, it is inevitable that much interaction between these two groups is bound to occur; indeed, the Great Commission demands that the true Christian do just this. All Christians have a duty to evangelize. But this intermixing in the everyday affairs of life also carries with it this particular danger: in the event that the Christian becomes careless, the process can reverse. In this case, the church does not Christianize the society so much as the church itself becomes paganized. Once this happens, the church begins to appear more promising to the unsaved man, and the end result is a church largely composed of unsaved people.

That this has happened to the church in previous times can hardly be denied. In many ages, the church has been careless and admitted large numbers of those who never really knew the Lord. The total number of reasons for the unsaved man desiring to enter the church could probably never be counted, though some of the more popular ones might include the respect of society, having deceived themselves into thinking they are Christians when they are not, or simply going because it seems like the "proper" thing to do. Likewise, it is hardly a secret that many clergymen have accepted their position not out of love for God, but because they saw the opportunity as a chance for an "easy living" (not that a pastor's job is easy, when it is done right). But whatever the reason, it is a fact that the unsaved man does often gain access to church membership, and even to positions of leadership within the church.

Considering the vast differences in thought between the saved and unsaved, it is obvious that such entrance by the unregenerate will produce serious effects in the church. The natural man remains in a state of rebellion against the Lord; therefore, his presence, especially in large quantities, results in a similar reaction in the collective church. The unregenerate man has no honest desire to please God at all, as he is blinded by the curse of sin, and totally unable to see or comprehend anything dealing with spiritual matters (I Cor. 2:14). As all unsaved men do, he places his own judgment ahead of the Lord's, and despises His authority.

Thus, when unsaved men enter a church, the end result is always a rejection of the authority of God, at least in some respect.

This rejection of authority can take many forms and appearances; but they all take the emphasis off of obedience to God, and place it on man, generally making human welfare the church's ultimate concern. It is therefore no coincidence that practically all modern heresies substitute a god who will cooperate with mankind in the attainment of humanistic goals, in the stead of the true God, before whom all must submit. From the unsaved man's point of view, the church can have no other useful purpose.

Generally, the first sign that this transition is taking place in a church is an open rejection of the Scriptures as the chief authority for the Christian. Since the Bible is in radical opposition to the goals of the natural man, he must seek to destroy its authority before he can attempt to make his own plans seem credible. Therefore, the true Christian must not only seek to obey the Scriptures himself, but also take note that there is no tendency in his church towards belittling them. For this must be the first step by the natural man to overthrow God's authority in the church.

Another result of unsaved men entering a church is a growing tolerance of sin. This, too, logically follows from the fact that they are in rebellion against God and despise His authority. Considering that they hold His Word in such low esteem, it is only natural that the unsaved man does not feel bound to obey it. Furthermore, the spiritual blindness which accompanies the unregenerate state may harden a man's heart to the point where he is not properly able to discern what is right or wrong in a given situation. In this case, he is bound to be tolerant of sin to some degree, simply because his natural mind cannot always perceive that a particular action is a sin.

Besides causing a shift in authority and a tolerance towards genuine sin, worldly elements in the church also generate apathy. This is because an unregenerate man does not genuinely consider obedience to God a significant matter. He fails to understand both his own need and helplessness, as well as the greatness and majesty of God. He is so overcome by worldly desires that he cannot honestly give the true God much time or effort. And even in the event that the worldly elements tend to be of a more active sort, their service tends to be just as worldly as they are. If they get involved at all, it will generally be to aid in some form of social cause.

Following this same type of pattern, another effect the unsaved man produces in the church is a bias towards the love and mercy of God, at the expense of a balanced emphasis on God's justice and hatred of sin. For if the unsaved man does not take sin seriously, then he obviously has no desire to listen to threats of suffering eternity in hell for his disobedience. Thus, the worldly elements attempt to generate a false concept of God which tends to be more favorable towards the present state of man. Rather than correct the problem in man, they attempt to change to a different God who approves of them just as they are.

That these statements are at least essentially correct can be seen quite clearly by turning to the Bible and noting how it portrays the unsaved man. They generally love to disregard God's law; they take sin lightly; and they almost always hold themselves in more esteem than they should. They often like to emphasize God's love for themselves totally out of relation with the facts, and ignore the fact that God will bring judgment on them for evil (Jeremiah 8:4-15, Jeremiah 6:13-15, Jer. 7:1-26, Ezek. 11:1-12, Ezek. 13:1-16).

An objection can be raised, of course, that just because these statements are essentially correct, that this does not prove that it is very much of a problem in the present-day church. But such an objection can hold little force. When we look about us and see churches financing terrorist operations and putting up abortion clinics, certainly even the most naive of Christians can see that something is seriously wrong. For while it is true that Christians can sin, and to a certain degree be ignorant of Christian principles, it is even more certain that a person led by the Holy Spirit could not rest his mind at ease while supporting many of the things which some churches do today. If anyone really has doubts concerning this matter, let him look at the many controversies which the church is presently engaged in. A few examples might be the ordination of women as leaders of the church when the Bible clearly indicates that it is wrong, the attempts to justify such things as divorce on non-Biblical grounds, and even the approval given to such things as adultery, fornication, and homosexuality by many liberal clergymen. These things are not merely insignificant differences in opinions by equally sincere Christians; they are conflicts between true Christianity and a false Christianity, a Christianity based on God's authority and one based on humanism, a conflict between those truly dedicated to God and those dedicated to Satan.

That unsaved men are abundant in today's churches can hardly be denied by any thinking man. The question is, What must we do to rid the church of this problem?

Many conservative churchmen, trying to cope with the massive problems of the churches, have attempted to produce reform by concentrating their efforts on the edification of the true believers, and stressing the importance of a close relationship with God. The idea is that if individual Christians will largely edify themselves, then the edification of the church as a whole will soon have to follow. But while such a relationship is indeed an important part of reform, as will soon be seen, it serves as a poor starting point, because of one major flaw: the unregenerate members (and there can be many) will not be affected by such a procedure at all. This plan works well so long as everyone in the church is already a Christian, but what happens when there are many unsaved "Christians" in the church? What happens when they make up the majority, or even dominate the leadership? In cases such as these, stressing the relationship of God and His authority to man won't solve the problem, because a large portion of the people are unresponsive. As a matter of fact, the natural man generally recoils strongly from the idea of a God who is totally sovereign and the final authority on all matters.

So we begin to see that stressing God's authority and disciplining our own lives as Christians is only part of reforming the church. Our goal is to give to God all authority in the church; but it is clear that many will not do this voluntarily. They would rather be free to do their own will, think their own way, and will not tolerate having their life style cramped by Biblical guidelines. God's law really means nothing to them, and they see no problem in overlooking any Scripture which stands in their way for a "free" (which generally means sin-filled) manner of living. These people are, of course, not really Christians at all, but counterfeit Christians who have entered the church for less than honorable reasons.

It must be understood that before the church can be cleansed, before we can hope to develop a more strongly disciplined church, this worldly influence must be removed. It is clear that so long as they remain in rebellion against God, they cannot accomplish anything pleasing to Him. They can only serve as a degenerative force. Therefore, the first step in any attempt at reform by the churches must be to try to remove these worldly elements. (By "worldly elements," we are referring of course only to those who are professing to be Christians when they are not, and are church members or leaders. We obviously are not seeking to ban unsaved people from attending services, as one major purpose of the church is evangelism. Unsaved people should be encouraged to attend, but should not be accepted as Christians.)

Attempting to stop Satan's influence in the church is futile, until we make a conscious effort to rid ourselves of his representatives within our ranks. For why is it that God has, so often throughout history, chosen persecution as the means of cleansing His church? To be sure, persecution does tend to strengthen the character of the true Christian, but doesn't the primary advantage of it lie in the fact that it drives out all of the worldly and half-hearted elements?

Every Christian should constantly seek to better his relationship with God; but until the church learns how to effectively respond to these outside forces, it will remain in its present state of confusion. How could it be otherwise, when we have spiritually regenerated and unregenerated under the same roof? As the Scriptures say, "Can two walk together except they be agreed?" (Amos 3:3) (KJV).

The church must therefore apply itself to the task of removing these unsaved persons. The true Christian may sin, but he has the ability to overcome it. The unsaved man cannot overcome his deficiency, because he likes it. He is therefore incorrigible and totally beyond help, unless God chooses to regenerate him. He has nothing to recommend him to either God or the church—he is spiritual garbage. And like all garbage, he must be thrown out if the house is to be made clean.

The Biblical Justification for Removal

It is true that statements such as these present to the Christian certain practical problems, not the least of which is man's inability to fully discern the spiritual state of another; but before we examine these practical considerations in the light of Scripture, let us first continue with the theological proofs of this matter, and show beyond all doubt that this is indeed what God would have us to do.

The thought of removing specific persons from the church may seem exceedingly harsh to many Christians of our day. They have grown up in an age of tolerance—an age in which it is regarded as acceptable to believe just about anything, so long as no harm to others will result. But such matters cannot be left to our own judgment; the true Christian's duty is to search Scripture, for only in the Bible can we find an answer based on absolute Truth.

Upon doing so, the Christian finds numerous verses pertaining to this question, a few examples of which might be these:

I Corinthians 5:9-13

I have written you in my letter not to associate with sexually immoral people—not at all meaning the people of this world who are immoral, or the greedy and swindlers, or idolaters. In that case you would have to leave this world. But now I am writing you that you must not associate with anyone who calls himself a brother but is sexually immoral or greedy, an idolater or a slanderer, a drunkard or a swindler. With such a man do not even eat.

What business is it of mine to judge those outside the church? Are you not to judge those inside? God will judge those outside. Expel the wicked man from among you. (NIV)

II Corinthians 6:14-18

Do not be yoked together with unbelievers. For what do righteousness and wickedness have in common? Or what fellowship can light have with darkness? What harmony is there between Christ and Belial? What does a believer have in common with an unbeliever? What agreement is there between the temple of God and idols? For we are the temple of the living God. As God has said: "I will live with them and walk with them, and I will be their God, and they will be my People."

Therefore come out from them and be separate, says the Lord. Touch no unclean thing, and I will receive you. I will be a Father to you, and you will be my sons and daughters, says the Lord Almighty. (NIV).

Matthew 18:15-17

If your brother sins against you, go and show him his fault, just between the two of you. If he listens to you, you have won your brother over. But if he will not listen, take

one or two others along, so that every matter may be established by the testimony of two or three witnesses. If he refuses to listen to them, tell it to the church; and if he refuses to listen even to the church, treat him as you would a pagan or a tax collector. (NIV).
II John 10, 11
If anyone comes to you and does not bring this teaching, do not take him into your house or welcome him. Anyone who welcomes him shares in his wicked work. (NIV).
Romans 16:17-18
I urge you, brothers, to watch out for those who cause divisions and put obstacles in your way that are contrary to the teaching you have learned. Keep away from them. For such people are not serving our Lord Christ, but their own appetites. By smooth talk and flattery they deceive the minds of naive people. (NIV).

Surely these passages provide clear testimony that the God of the Bible expects His people to remain separate from those who despise Him, and that they must deal with these men accordingly when they contaminate His church.

To those who truly love God and want to obey His commandments, these instructions from Scripture will undoubtedly suffice in convincing them of this truth. But in all fairness to those who might oppose us on this issue, and for the further instruction of those whose knowledge of the Christian faith is yet minimal, it is only right that we confront the two objections which most certainly will be hurled at us from the more "liberal" quarters of the church. These two objections might be stated briefly as thus:

(1) It violates the Biblical commandments to love one another when we insist on the removal of these persons from the church, and
(2) It is wrong for anyone to judge the actions of another, something which we must do in order to justify their removal.

Since either of these objections might at first appear to have some Biblical support, it is important that we examine them more closely. Upon doing so, we shall demonstrate that both of these lines of reasoning, as common as they are in the church today, are not founded upon the Word of God at all, but are based solely upon the superficial relativism so popular in contemporary Western thought. In so doing, we will be able to prove our point all the more clearly.

Love and the Necessity of Intolerance

The first objection which is sure to arise in response to these statements concerning the removal of the unsaved is that such action would violate God's commandments to love one another. Our opponents on this issue are sure to remind us that all of the laws and commandments are summarized under the more general command to love God with all our heart and our neighbor as ourself. They would therefore have us conclude that our responsibility to love these people should overshadow our judgments concerning their spiritual state.

The Christian must use caution at this point, for while the summary of the law and the prophets may lie in loving God and our neighbor as ourself, this in itself cannot be taken as the basis for either a reform movement or as a foundation for the church in general. Many have fallen into this error and plunged their churches or denominations into a state of degeneration, on the grounds that "love" is supreme and that any law or commandment which stands in its way can be safely ignored. But those who so rashly throw Biblical authority out the window are in for a disappointment—for those who think they must disobey Scripture in order to show true love are only deceiving themselves.

Where they err is in their mistaken concept of what constitutes "love." They have attempted to make this a subjective term, its meaning defined by their own personal preference. By so doing, they can justify virtually any sinful act they wish. They need only point out that their actions are in some way benefitting someone, and they are led to conclude that what they are doing must be the will of God. Hence, we have many liberal church organizations now supporting terrorist groups, all operating under the guise of "Christian love," in that they are attempting to help their "brethren" achieve "liberation." So long as they reserve for themselves the right to define just what constitutes "Christian love," they can justify any number of absurdities.

But true Christian love is not a warm feeling based on the will of man; it is found rather in a desire to obey God and follow His commandments. When Christ said that to love was the sum of the law, He did not in the least imply that love is above the commandments—only that it is defined by them. This is clearly what He had in mind, for in John 14, Jesus says, "Whoever has my commands and obeys them, he is the one who loves me" (vs. 21) (NIV). True love is not a simple-minded infatuation, or even a sincere attempt to be "nice" or concerned about those around us, apart from obedience to God's Word. For only God can truly define what constitutes love; we cannot leave such a term free to be interpreted by the warped and sinful mind of men.

Hence, while the primary commandment given to the Christian may be to love, even this can be defined only by the authority on which the church is based. Any true love must be in accordance with Biblical principles. And any true reform movement must look first of all to this authority, and not be dependent upon an undefined feeling.

It is at this point that many well-meaning Christians have been led astray. There are many instances in which God's definition of love clashes radically with what the natural mind would conceive of. Take, for example, the current trend against inflicting discipline on children. Out of "love" for the child, the parents would never resort to spanking him; yet, God says that any man who spares the rod from his son hates him (Prov. 13:24). Another example might be the trend in many churches toward regarding homosexuality as socially acceptable. The idea is that it is wrong to reject a person simply because his opinion of what's right and wrong differs, and therefore that "love" demands they be allowed entrance to the church. And yet, time and again, God tells us that homosexuality is totally unacceptable, and that anyone involved in it will not enter His Kingdom (I Cor. 6:9, 10; Lev. 20:13, Lev. 18:22, and Romans 1:25-32). The Christian must consider whether true love consists of demanding repentance from an individual otherwise destined for eternity in Hell, or of providing for the conveniences of this life by offering him an unrepentant church membership which leaves him in a state of damnation. Surely careful consideration on this matter will leave any Christian convinced that it is both dangerous and foolish to demonstrate any form of "love" which is in opposition to God's law.

Our concept of love cannot be based on our own judgment, but must be derived from the Bible. Such an approach may not always seem appropriate by worldly standards, but that does not excuse us from performing the required operation, as God insists that we love our neighbor as ourselves. This love must be shown whether the action involved seems proper by our standards or not.

In reference to the subject that we are presently addressing, it should be understood that when the situation presents itself, the only loving thing which can sometimes be done to those in the church who refuse to submit to God's authority is to expel them. We can see that this is true whether we examine the situation from the perspective of the person, from the perspective of the church, or from the perspective of God Himself.

From the perspective of the rebellious man, the obvious danger lies in the fact that if he is not confronted, he will be tempted to continue in sin. Why should he stop, if no one is even willing to express disapproval? It is therefore the church's duty to rebuke such men, in the hope that they will show true signs of spiritual life and repent. But if the man is obstinate, and insists on continuing in sin, the church must apply stronger discipline, lest the man be forever lost. In cases such as these, excommunication must be applied for the man's own good—for if the church backs down and allows him to remain a member while in rebellion, he will never experience true repentance.

The objection can be made that the person may only get angry and leave the church altogether, whether an offer to return upon proof of repentance is offered or not. But it must be remembered that if this is the case, and the reproof was not given in a hypocritical or self-righteous manner, he was apparently not saved to begin with, or else he would acknowledge God's sovereignty over his life and submit. Hence, nothing has been lost; for by ignoring his problem, he may remain a church member, but he is still in a state of damnation, and under these circumstances would probably never be saved, either.

It is essential that the church be kept clear of sin, and the removal of unsaved persons is a must. Leaving them in the church as members is not doing them a favor—it's robbing them of perhaps their only chance of experiencing salvation when they are refused this disciplinary measure. This is not unloving or hateful, but indeed a display of love in itself, in that in forcing their withdrawal from the church, they are duly warned of their deficient spiritual state. As a result, at least some may truly repent and be saved, whereas if left alone in the church they would probably have been eternally lost.

When viewed from the aspect of the church, it becomes even more clear why the unsaved person must be removed from the congregation: it prevents the other members from being contaminated with the rebellious man's sins. Sin is like a cancer, or as Paul says, "A little leaven leaveneth the whole lump" (I Cor. 5:6) (KJV). If allowed into a church, it can spread rapidly, affecting the whole membership. Once it is detected, it should always be dealt with immediately, for the sake of the other members as well as the individual himself.

The power of a bad example is too often ignored or underemphasized in the church, but God does not take such matters lightly. He cautions us in the Scriptures to remove those in the church who lead wicked lives, lest they lead others also astray (I Cor. 5). Indeed, the Apostle Paul sees such great danger here, that he forbids the Christian to even associate with such men (I Cor. 5:11).

Thirdly, the Christian must also recognize that this rule of putting out those who despise God's authority is not merely a request, but a divine commandment. God is not asking for consideration on the matter, but for obedience. And no wonder—for God has created us solely to bring glory to Himself; but what glory is there in having the most wicked men on the face of the earth calling themselves by His name? Those who truly love God will see immediately that this is the most important reason of all for expelling those in the church who do not belong to Him—to keep them from bringing disgrace down on His precious Son.

Thus, we see that true Christian love in no way forbids us from removing unsaved men from the church; rather, it testifies to the very necessity of such action. Those who find in the word "love" an excuse to allow unsaved men to overrun God's church are not thinking in terms of Scripture, but have put their own judgment ahead of the Lord's.

"Judge not, that ye be not judged."
(Matthew 7:1) (KJV)

The second objection certain to be brought against us in this matter is that we do not have the authority to judge others. Our opponents will undoubtably proceed to prove their point by quoting Matthew 7:1, which says, "Judge not, that ye be not judged." (KJV). They find in this, and similar verses, proof that no one has the right to make judgments concerning the character or actions of another.

But this notion is easily refuted; for if Christ intended this as they interpret it, then how are we to determine just who the "dogs" and "swine" are in verse six of this same chapter? Likewise, in verses 15 and 16, Jesus proceeds to give us instructions on how to judge whether a person belongs to Him or not. Surely those who interpret the first verse of this chapter to mean that we are forbidden to make character judgments concerning one another have interpreted it wrongly.

The purpose of verses such as Matthew 7:1, Romans 2:1, and James 4:11-12, is not to promote anarchy in the church, as some contemporary churchmen are eager to imagine, but is rather just an ordinary application of the Golden Rule; that is, we should not condemn others, just as we would not want to be condemned. It is clear from the context of these verses that Christ and the Apostles are referring primarily to a tendency to criticize and condemn others, sinful acts which arise from a sense of pride and self-righteousness. But those who take this to mean that it is also wrong to rebuke others, and to take action when necessary, to bring or restore them to God, are trying to read too much into these verses.

When we examine such verses as I Tim. 5:20, "Those who sin are to be rebuked publicly, so that the others may take warning" (NIV), Titus 1:13, "Therefore, rebuke them sharply so that they will be sound in the faith" (NIV), I Corin, 5:12, 13, and Matthew 7:15-20, it is clear that the Christian must sometimes make judgments concerning those about him; this is indeed his duty. What separates this action from the sinful acts described in the previous verses is basically two things: (1) the intention of the person making the judgment, and (2) the authority on which the person has based his judgment. It is primarily these factors which determine whether a judgment was properly made or not.

The first factor, the intention of the heart, is of primary importance, as judging out of a wrong motivation is what the Scriptures are chiefly speaking against here. When we note a professing Christian committing a sin, there are two things which can motivate us to confront him: a sincere desire to help him overcome his weakness, or a desire to belittle him and make ourselves look better by comparison. We should hope that our motives would always fall into the first category, but it is indeed all too often true that when we make judgments concerning one another, it is mainly to criticize.

It will be noted that in every single verse which states that we are not to judge our brother, without exception, it is in the sense of condemning and criticizing, perhaps rashly, and probably hypocritically. We have no excuse for attempting to exalt ourselves over anyone else as their judge, and expecting them to conform to our expectations. Because we ourselves have sinned, we have no right to condemn anyone.

However, because we are not to judge others in this sense, which is a sin, it does not hold therefore that we are not to reprove others, which is a necessary duty, and may even be a means of saving a soul from eternal death. Note that in each of the verses which state or imply that we are to judge our brethren, it is always done in the spirit of love. It is not because of a condemning, self-righteous bitterness that we rebuke our brother, but because we seek to help him. Even if he refuses the help, and must be expelled from the church, it is still from a spirit of love that this must be done—a love for the good and spiritual welfare of all the other members of the church.

Thus we have here a situation where an action could be judged as either good or evil, depending solely upon the motive. The Christian is strictly forbidden to make judgments about a brother when his motive is based on impure intentions, but he is not only justified in confronting him, but is commanded to do so, when his primary desire is to help restore the brother to God. This is likewise true concerning the professing Christian who is not saved; even if he must be excommunicated, this should be done out of a love and zeal for God's church, and the spiritual welfare of the man—not out of hatred and self-righteousness.

The second point that we must consider here is the authority on which our judgment is based. For people can often misjudge others while having the best of intentions themselves. If their judgments are not based solidly on Scripture, but upon their own beliefs or standards, then their judgments can easily be in error. And even in the event that their own standards are not totally in error, they still have no right to judge others by them. The Christian's duty is to think after the thoughts of God, and to think in terms of God's desires, not his own. The Christian must therefore submit his own reasoning and standards to the Word of God.

It is a strong tendency in humans to want to either add or subtract our own opinions to God's Word, and these can easily color our judgments. The list of "laws" added to the Scriptures by some groups, and the list of true commandments "explained away" by others, makes it clear that many in the church do judge at least partially by their own standards, rather than God's. The problem here, however, is not always a critical heart, as they may have the best of intentions in such cases. The problem is that they are judging others by a system based on their own opinions; opinions which, we might add, God has never asked for. Thus, the problem is not necessarily one of a consciously wrong motivation, so much as one of a misplaced authority. The Christian must beware of this tendency, and make certain that his judgments are Scripturally sound.

But aside from these possible errors, the fact remains that the Christian is instructed to make certain judgments concerning those who are members of the church. The society in which we live at the present time is highly relativistic, and it is therefore rather unfashionable to do this. But the Scriptures are clear, and the true Christian must obey. Just as it is our duty not to judge wrongly, it likewise is our duty to discipline, and to deal with those in the church who hate God.

In conclusion, judgments concerning others in the church should not be made rashly, but only after we have looked within ourselves. The fact that what we find there may not yet be perfect does not, however, forbid us from making character judgments concerning the actions of others. The true Christian must make certain that he judges only with a right heart, and bases his judgments solely upon the Scriptures; but these restrictions do not nullify his duty to keep God's church pure. Because unsaved men do enter the church, and because they do produce only harmful effects, we are not only given the authority to remove them, but must in fact do so.

Chapter 4

Coping with the Unregenerate Influence in the Church—Part II: Practical Considerations

The course of action suggested in the preceeding chapter for coping with unregenerate members in the church is not without difficulties. From a purely theological perspective, the removal of the unsaved is indeed a valid principle, but certain problems will invariably arise in any attempt to enforce it, due to man's various limitations. It is therefore essential that we examine the most important of these practical considerations, at least briefly, and note the effect they will have on the Christian's ability to perform this task.

1. Man's Inability to Fully Discern the Spiritual State of Another

The first point that the Christian must consider is man's inability to fully discern the spiritual state of another. For since man possesses only a finite and rather limited mental capacity, no one can truly see into the heart of another person with full understanding. Hence, any judgments which we make concerning one another will be based on an incomplete knowledge of that person, a factor which greatly enhances the possibility of an erroneous conclusion. This obviously generates a most serious problem, for it is of little value to recognize the necessity of removing the unregenerate from the church, if we cannot accurately determine who they are.

It is not always possible to state unconditionally that a person is unregenerate as a result of his outward actions alone. For while some such men may indeed commit such gross sin as to leave little doubt, this is not always true by any means. This matter is further complicated by the fact that even the true Christian will display worldly characteristics on occasion. No one, saved or unsaved, is totally immune from the effects of sin in this life.

Therefore, we cannot always rely on outward actions alone as a basis for determining this matter. How then can the Christian, under these circumstances, identify and separate the true believer from the false?

Because God is fully aware of man's many shortcomings, and the problems which can ultimately result from them, He has provided us with some simple rules to follow. We find them set forth in Matthew 18:15-17, which says,

> If your brother sins,[1] go and show him his fault, just between the two of you. If he listens to you, you have won your brother over. But if he will not listen, take one or two others along, so that every matter may be established by the testimony of two or three witnesses. If he refuses to listen to them, tell it to the church; and if he refuses to listen even to the church, treat him as you would a pagan or a tax collector. (Matthew 18:15-17) (NIV)

Therefore, when we are sinned against by another professing Christian, or witness such a sin, our first duty is to go directly to the person and confront him, in the hopes that he will show true spiritual life and repent. The humanistic influence in our culture might label this as "judging," and tell us to do otherwise, but God's word is clear, and no Christian has the right to neglect this duty. A person who sins should be confronted with it. If the person still shows no spiritual response, we take two or more witnesses along to emphasize the gravity of the situation and to establish a case. If repentance is still not produced, we turn the matter over to the elders of the church. (It should be noted, however, in cases of gross offense committed by an elder or minister, that the case is to be brought directly to the church, that others may take warning from his example—I Timothy 5:20.)

The point to note here is that the church is not instructed to remove a person for falling into disobedience (which all men do), per se, but for possessing a rebellious spirit which prevents him from coming to repentance. This is, of course, to a large extent what separates the saved from the unsaved; for whereas all men commit sin, only the true Christian will ever honestly repent of it, as even this factor of repentance is a gift from God included in salvation (II Tim. 2:25). The most common response from those who do not possess this gift will be anger. Thus, the process outlined in Matthew 18 effectively separates those who will submit to the authority of God from those who will not, exactly what we desire.

But note also that this passage makes no distinction as to whether the person is saved or not; it orders that all be treated the same. It might seem unlikely that a true Christian would go through all of these warnings without repenting, but in a backslidden condition, it might be possible. And in this fact we find the beauty of this whole system—for while it was demonstrated previously that the Christian does have the authority and duty to make certain judgments concerning others in the church, we can now see that he does not necessarily have to go so far as to make a total judgment concerning the man's salvation; that can be left to God. All we have to do is make certain judgments based on the man's actions, and follow the proper Biblical guidelines. The man's willingness or unwillingness to submit to the authority of God will then be brought out into the open.

We can see that this whole plan that God has devised is more or less based on a "cause-and-effect" principle. We cannot always determine what is in the heart of another person, but we do know that anyone whose heart has been regenerated will emanate certain effects. If the effects are not there, then neither is the changed heart. As Christ said, "You will know them by their fruits."

The objection can be raised, of course, that some people in the church might conceivably live a life of sin while not under our scrutiny, and yet, put on a performance in our presence which would fool even the most critical saint. That this objection is valid, there can be no doubt; however, in practical terms, it really has little impact upon the situation. It is true that such people, though certainly not deceiving God, can deceive us; but if they are acting so much like a Christian that we cannot tell the difference anyway, then they are at least no serious detriment to the church, since they are also encouraging obedience to God in an outward way. They may be condemned themselves, but they do not directly serve as a bad influence for others.

Neither should the Christian be overly concerned about the possibility of a true Christian (in a backslidden state) being removed from the church. For once he repents, there is nothing to prevent him from being reaccepted into the fellowship. Indeed, this disciplinary measure not only may wake up a "sleepy" Christian, but might even result in the salvation of some of the unsaved persons when they are chastised in this way. We see this demonstrated in the letters of Paul to the Corinthians. In the first letter, Paul tells them to remove "that wicked man" from their presence (Chapter 5), but in the second letter (Chapter 2), congratulates them for reaccepting the man after such discipline brought him to (or back to) Christ. All churches should operate according to this policy—our desire is not only to keep God's church pure, but if possible, to also help the offender become right with God.

2. The "Nominal" Christian

One serious problem which must be dealt with, however, is the fact that most unsaved, worldly persons in the churches are apathetic. It is relatively easy to see the danger that can result from a man who openly denies Biblical authority, or the problems that can ultimately arise when gross sin is tolerated within a congregation. But most of the worldly persons in the church do not do these things—they are "respectable" people, people who come to church nearly every Sunday, but do little else. Christianity is basically a one-hour-a-week affair for them.

On the surface, these people might seem harmless. But we cannot allow ourselves to be deceived on this point, for no matter how persuasive the argument for the "nominal" Christian might be, it is not Biblical. The Bible teaches that truly regenerated Christians are a new creature, a new creature dedicated to leaving behind the old sinful life, and striving for complete perfection of the new, through Christ Jesus. No where is there any suggestion that the true Christian will be apathetic or lazy. The true Christian has been called by God to a life of holiness for Him.

The danger present from these people should be relatively clear in our age, for they have been rather numerous in the past generation. They generate apathy, often serve as bad examples for real Christians, leading them into sin, and also discredit the church on occasion by professing Christianity and yet living a life, if not of gross sin, then at least in a worldly manner. These "harmless" unsaved members are not really harmless at all, but must be likewise removed.

The removal of these people, however, can be a troublesome situation. The difficulty lies in the fact that because they don't do anything, it is difficult to explain why they should be removed. We must note, also, that God has never commanded the removal of apathetic persons, as such, so much as gross offenders.

The probable reason that we have not been commanded to remove those who seem "apathetic" is that we cannot "know them by their fruits," if we don't have enough fruits to make an adequate judgment. The fact that a person might only come to church for an hour a week, for instance, and not take part in any other activities, does not prove in the least that the person is apathetic or nonspiritual, any more than a person who takes part in everything is guaranteed to be a true Christian. Differences in personalities, and the fact that a person's faith can be expressed in many ways, makes it dangerous to assume a person is unsaved because of failure to take part in certain activities. The most reliable sign of an unregenerate state we are to observe is an unwillingness to obey and repent. Until we find such an attitude clearly displayed, we have no right to consider them lost.

Therefore, when we encounter such situations, perhaps the best course of action is to follow the same basic plan that God did when the Israelites didn't want to go into the Promised Land. He simply raised a new generation who would be faithful, and waited for the older generation to die off. By this, we mean that if more caution is used in allowing in only new members who show a true dedication to the Lord, eventually a higher level of dedication in the church as a whole will begin to show, as the older, apathetic members eventually leave (by whatever means). Such a system would require that the elders (or minister or examining committee, as the case may be) take extra time and care in examining each candidate for membership. Also, a trial membership period might be considered, which would allow the church leaders a greater chance to observe the spiritual stature of the person involved. Any such system, however, should always be set up to observe how the new Christian responds toward the authority of God's Word and any necessary discipline—and not be based on their participation in church activities.

Any such process, of course, will take time, and requires patience. A church does not degenerate overnight; neither will it be reformed overnight. But such efforts will eventually pay off, as those who do not love the Lord leave.

3. When the Unregenerate Gain Positions of Authority in the Church

Certainly one of the most irritating problems for any reformer is to encounter a situation where unsaved men occupy the positions of authority within a church denomination. Surprisingly, this is not an uncommon occurance in this particular age, especially in some "mainline" and "united" churches. This, of course, makes the case much more difficult to handle, for the final board to which the reformer must appeal is on the side of the enemy.

It is clear that the progression outlined in the previous sections for dealing with unsaved men in the church depends to a large extent upon the integrity of the church leadership (on both an individual and a denominational basis). It would obviously be of no avail to have a man brought before a board of elders for having committed a gross sin, when the elders themselves approve of such things, or even encourage it. This being the case, we can see that allowing unregenerate men into the leadership of a church is probably the worst mistake that we can make, for once they have authority over the church, it is virtually impossible to correct the situation.

Indeed, coping with unregenerate men in the church is always a situation where "an ounce of prevention is worth a pound of cure." Keeping unsaved men from the membership is really not too difficult in the majority of cases; getting them out once they are in is another matter altogether. The most frightening aspect of this problem is that once a few unsaved men are allowed to enter, it can easily result in a "runaway" condition that is almost impossible to stop. That is, once we compromise by making a church comfortable for unsaved men by tolerating sin and not making their degenerate natures stand out, we encourage two things.

(1) We encourage more unsaved people to join; unsaved men who wish to join a church (for whatever reason), will clearly prefer a church where their degenerate state will not be brought into the limelight, and
(2) We encourage the Christians to leave, and especially encourage other Christians who might consider membership there to go elsewhere.

As more unsaved enter the church, the situation continually becomes better and better for the unsaved, and continually worse for the true Christian. Once this runaway condition starts, it is just a matter of time before the unsaved make up the majority of the membership. If this condition exists in enough churches within a denomination, they will soon also control the denominational leadership positions.

Some persons might be inclined to scoff at the idea that a majority of the leadership within a church denomination could be unregenerate. But let them consider the way in which some churches have consistently sided with non-Biblical objectives, supported terrorist programs (or as they call them, "missionary programs"), how they have repeatedly encouraged life styles and practices in direct opposition to the dictates of God's Word, and have despised God's authority and Person in general. These practices are not due to insignificant differences of opinion concerning what's right and what's wrong, because the One from whom their opinions differ is the Almighty Lord and Creator of the universe, the one to whom they swear their allegiance and obedience when they become Christians. Neither are these episodes the result of occasional "mistakes," because most of these things have been done again and again, with no signs as of yet that they are even willing to acknowledge that an error has been made. The only sensible conclusion that can be drawn concerning these particular churches is that the majority of the denominational leadership approves of these actions, in spite of the fact that God has repeatedly stated that it is wrong. And since a true Christian, that is, one who has been regenerated by God's Spirit, wants to follow His every decree (and is miserable if he doesn't), we need say no more to demonstrate that it is possible for the majority of a church leadership to be unsaved. The testimony of some churches about us is too glaring to be denied.

How, then, is the Christian to cope with a situation such as this?
There seems to be three routes that he can go:

(1) he can do nothing, and live with the corruption as best he can, or
(2) he can attempt to regain control of the leadership for the true Christians, or

(3) he can leave the corrupt denomination and seek fellowship with true Christians in another church.

The first choice is probably the one that most of God's people have followed in the church's past history (in both the Old and New Testament churches). The idea of doing nothing and accepting the situation as it is seems to appeal to many people. Unfortunately, it doesn't appeal to God, and this choice has generally resulted in God bringing persecution or other undesirable effects on them in order that they might be forced to shun their indifference. Hopefully, a better choice than this one can be found.

Of the remaining alternatives, the choice between these two routes can probably best be made by a careful evaluation of the condition of the denominational leadership. If this leadership as a whole is still somewhat faithful, remaining there and seeking to have the leadership of a particular church removed is a feasible plan. If the leaders of such a church do not respond to offenses against God, and refuse to discipline offenders, the denominational heads can be called in for support. And even in the event that the denominational leaders are partially corrupt, there still may be a good chance of saving that denomination if such corrupt men do not yet hold very much strength.

But if, as in some denominations today, unsaved men clearly have firm control over the denominational leadership, and, perhaps just as important, have control over the seminaries, the best route to take is probably for the true Christians to leave and go to another denomination where God's Word is held in high esteem. The idea of "staying behind to fight it," even in the face of overwhelming odds and when heavily outnumbered, always has a more noble sound to it than that of "running away." In practice, however, most such attempts will result in failure. What we must keep in mind is that God's primary purpose in such matters is that His people be kept separate from the world—this is what is truly important. The fact that an old apostate church may exist for a time, pretending to belong to Him, is of little consequence. For even in the most degenerate of churches, it is usually the true Christians, however naive they might be, who are providing the main support. Once such an organization is deprived of these true Christians, it generally will not stand for long.

Some might wish to contest this statement, on the ground that it has not always been true that after a reform movement the old corrupt church just faded away. Probably the best example of this is the Roman Catholic Church; even after having been assailed by the strongest reform movement in the church's history (which, incidently, occurred by separation), it is still alive and well over 400 years later. But we must keep in mind two points here. The first is that a large percentage of Christians did stay behind in the Roman Church. It might seem obvious today that the Roman teachings had little to do with Biblical Christianity, but we must remember that the masses at that time had little education, few Bibles, and knew little about what Christianity did teach other than what the priests taught them. This is obviously a different case than from a person of our age who has been trained to read, has a Bible at his disposal, and refuses to read or obey it. Secondly, the Roman Church of that age does not truly exist today, anyhow. It may have the same name, and roughly the same form of government, but it has repeatedly been forced to compromise with Protestantism, and true Christianity in general, in order to survive into this age. The Roman Catholic Church of the 16th century could not survive in the 20th century; that system existed and depended on techniques that are not practical in our society.

Thus, separating from the old, corrupt church and joining one which truly honors God is often the only practical course open when the entire denomination is apostate; this is especially effective when it is carried out in large numbers, or entire churches decide to break free. Those who stay behind in a degenerate church, despite the fact that God has given no indication that He intends to reform it, should also consider the following:

(1) Any gifts or offerings that are given in the additional time that they stay can be used for any number of ungodly purposes.
(2) While remaining in a degenerate denomination for some time longer, they are expending much energy and effort fighting the actions of the liberal groups that could otherwise be used in more constructive activities for Christ.
(3) While the reformers are occupied trying to restore proper Biblical teachings in the church and Sunday School, their children and grandchildren are having their faith and morals undermined by those who are opposed to such reform in the church, both through

the Sunday School and other means.
(4) The Bible teaches separation from unbelief; this is a command, not an option.

Hence, the Christian must not allow himself to spend years of his time, money, and effort on a lost cause. God is always going to keep a portion of the church on earth pure for Himself, but this is often through separation from the old, as in the Protestant Reformation.

But let us keep in mind that such situations as these only arise in the first place because of continued disobedience and apathy towards disciplining those who corrupt the church, and allowing the unsaved to enter at all. God's plan for maintaining purity in His church is summarized in Matthew 18:15-17; if this were consistently obeyed, these more extreme situations would never arise. It is only because of our own tolerance, tolerance which God forbids, that the church can get into such a condition that these few verses won't handle the situation.

The Christian must beware of any display of tolerance toward sin in the church. The growth of secular humanism in our culture, together with the accompanying relativistic concepts, have set forth "tolerance" as though it were the greatest of virtues. While it may be true that the opposite extreme has shown itself to be dangerous, that does not guarantee that this extreme is any better. The Christian must remember that the Word of God is to be his guide, not the word of his culture. Tolerance displayed toward anything is "good" only inasmuch as God's Word says it is.

Many will undoubtably be offended in any attempt to correct this problem, but the Christian's primary concern is not to please men, but the Lord. God looks with favor on those who are zealous to do His will—not on those who cowardly remain silent in the face of opposition under the pretense of "keeping peace".

We read in Numbers 25:1-13, of how Israel was led astray to idol worship by the Moabite people. When a man of Israel sinned by bringing one of the Moabite girls into the camp, Phinehas (Aaron's grandson) grabbed a spear, rushed after them into the man's tent, and drove the spear through both of them. The society in which we presently live would undoubtably look upon this as a most ungodly and terrible thing to do—an act of which God would have to disapprove.

But did God rebuke or punish Phinehas for this action? Quite the contrary, He approved of it very strongly, and praised him for it! As God replied, "Phinehas son of Eleazar, the son of Aaron, the priest, has turned my anger away from the Israelites; for he was as zealous as I am for my honor among them, so that in my zeal I did not put an end to them . . . " (NIV). This passage shows just how strongly God approves of those who act out of true zeal for His honor, even if the action required might seem somewhat contrary to our standard social norm. The standard norm of this particular society seems to be one of tolerance, but this is not necessarily true of God's Kingdom.

In conclusion, we must remember that our goal in reform is to eliminate from the church any forces which despise the authority of God. Since all unsaved men fall into this category, the true believers must attempt to remain separate from them, by whatever means necessary. If we cannot get them out of our old churches, then we must start new churches; we can never allow ourselves to be content with any church which is tolerant of sin. Both man and the church were created for communion with God, and sin destroys that communion. For the church to display tolerance towards the one thing that can separate her from her God would be the very height of stupidity.

Chapter 5

The Second Condition of Reform: God's Authority in the Christian Life

The second condition of reform is concerned with the response of the true Christian to the authority of God. For while the Christian, unlike his unregenerate counterpart, desires to obey God, this does not in itself guarantee that he will do so. Regeneration does not result in instant perfection; it is just the beginning of the Christian life. This being the case, the next logical step in reform is to map out a course by which the truly saved man can proceed to grow towards perfection. (It is obvious, of course, that not every Christian will attempt to follow this as he should. But certainly every member of the church must be given the opportunity to work out a relationship with the Lord on his own. Discipline inflicted by others, discussed in the next chapter, must, by the dictates of general decency itself, be held in abeyance until necessity requires its intervention.)

Perfection, the goal of the Christian life, was defined as absolute obedience to God. Thus, at this stage of reform, the Christian's primary concern must be to concentrate on making God's authority dominant in his own life. This obedience is not rendered in an attempt to "buy" salvation, of course, as that has been purchased by the blood of Christ. Please understand that we are not trying to make ourselves "righteous" in God's sight by our obedience, but rather, we desire to obey because He has already made us righteous. The Christian must never think that he is "justifying" himself by such obedience. But it has always been man's chief end to live with, and for the glory of God, and it is still his chief end. So if we owed Him obedience before, for creating us and giving us life, then we certainly owe Him obedience now that He has bought back our souls at such a costly price. Thus, in living the true Christian life, we must remember that the highest state to which a Christian can aspire is absolute conformity and submission to the authority of God; that is, perfection (Matt. 5:48).

Now, in his quest to achieve this goal, there are clearly two things which the Christian needs in order to render proper obedience to God. One thing that is needed is a knowledge of God's will, for it is clearly impossible to obey if we don't know what we are supposed to be doing. But this knowledge is not enough in itself. For knowledge alone does not motivate us to obedience, and even a knowledge of God's law put into action may not be pleasing to God if the motivation is wrong. The Pharisees were highly motivated to obey God's law, and they knew it very well, but their motivation was only to glorify themselves, rather than the Lord (Matt. 23:1-7). Thus, there are essentially two requirements that must be met if a man's actions are to glorify God:

(1) we must have a heart right toward God, that we desire to obey for His glory; and
(2) we must have a knowledge of His will, so that we will do what He wants.

Let us examine each of these points in turn.

Our Motivation for Living the True Christian Life

It was pointed out earlier that the unsaved man could not please God with his "good works," because his heart was wrong. Even if he possessed a knowledge of what God expected of him and did it in an outward manner, his obedience would be unacceptable. Therefore, we must conclude that it is not just the obedience itself that God wants, but also the desire to submit to Him, and the desire to please Him, which generates the obedience for His glory. No act of submission counts for anything in the sight of God without this (Matthew 23).

Once we understand this point, then it is clear that the Christian's first step in his quest for holiness must be to make certain that his own heart is right with God. But just how is he to do this? Just what does it mean to have a "heart right towards God," and why is it that only those who have been regenerated can do this?

The answer to those questions can be found by looking no further than the very first and most important commandment given to us by our Lord, "Love the Lord your God with all your heart, and with all your soul and with all your mind and with all your strength" (Mark 12:30) (NIV). Clearly, the reason the unsaved man cannot have a heart right towards God is because he does not love Him. Indeed, the Scriptures call the unregenerate man an "enemy" of God (Romans 5:10). But in the process of salvation, God draws those whom He has chosen to save to Christ, and takes away their hatred of Himself by giving them a totally new nature (II Corin. 5:17; John 6:44; John 3:3, Titus 3:5; Col. 2:13). This does not mean that the love for God given in regeneration is fully mature—but the seedling is planted. The rest of the Christian's life, and his entire quest for sanctification, is to a large extent only the process of learning how to love God.

Now, it must be understood that when the Scriptures speak of love towards God, they are not necessarily referring to what the world would often consider love. That our love may include some form of emotional content is fine. But when the Bible speaks of love towards God, we find that Christian love must manifest itself, at least primarily, in a desire to please the Lord. The Apostle John tells us, "And this is love: that we walk in obedience to his commands" (II John 6) (NIV) and again, Jesus says, "Whoever has my commands and obeys them, he is the one who loves me" (John 14:21) (NIV). Thus, we see that true love must motivate us to submit to the authority of God. And since this is our chief duty in life, this explains why to love God with all of our heart, soul, and mind is the greatest commandment; for to obey this commandment automatically results in proper submission. Therefore, the goal of love and the goal of the church as a whole are one and the same: that God be glorified.

These concepts of love and submission to the authority of God are so hopelessly intertwined that any attempt to separate or isolate them must result in failure. Proper submission to God's authority requires love, or else our obedience will not honor Him; but any attempt to express love apart from submission to God's Word must ultimately result in it taking on a relativistic character, which will lead us away from both God and true love. (This was the error noted earlier, concerning the admission of homosexuals into the church under the pretense of "love.") Thus, love must lead us to submit to the Lord, but proper submission depends upon love to make it acceptable. It is clear then that a true love for God, and proper submission to His authority, are so deeply dependent upon one another that neither can be expressed independently.

But the Christian must keep in mind that love is not the goal in itself, but only a necessary means of motivation to achieve our true goal: submission to God in such a way as to bring Him honor. For if love were the goal in itself, we would need to be nothing other than "loving" to be perfect. But true love should result not only in our having love for God and one another, but should also generate and motivate us to such qualities as righteousness, justice, and all of the other "moral characteristics" which God possesses. We can only conclude, therefore, that our chief duty in this regard is to glorify God through submission with a right heart, and that love towards God is an essential part of the recipe.

How, then, are we to generate this love for God, this desire to please Him? The truth of the matter is, we can't "generate" it. Man must depend upon God to give it to him, and he must depend on Him to make it grow. Only as the Holy Spirit comes upon us and works in our hearts can we successfully overcome the sin in our lives. Thus, we see once again that our spiritual regeneration and growth are totally dependent upon the grace of God, bestowed solely on account of Christ's intercession for us (Eph. 2:4-10).

But from the human point of view, there are some things that the Christian can do to encourage the growth of this love. Just as God gives a flower the ability to grow, and yet gives us the privilege of watering and fertilizing it, so He allows us to take part in this. We are too weak to develop a love for God ourselves, hounded as we are by the nature of sin. Even the tiny faith that we have is a gift of God (Eph. 2:8). But we can strive to master a pattern of thought which is conducive to the growth of this love.

The Scriptures point out, in many places, the frame of mind the Christian should seek to maintain. The essence of the teaching of all of these verses, however, is that we put the desires of God and our neighbor before our own. Paul called himself a "servant" of Christ (Romans 1:1; Phil. 1:1, Titus 1:1). Christ also instructed us to think of ourselves in this way:

> Suppose one of you had a servant plowing or looking after the sheep. Would he say to the servant when he comes in from the field, "Come along now and sit down to eat?" Would he not rather say, "Prepare my supper, get yourself ready and wait on me while I eat and drink; after that you may eat and drink"? Would he thank the servant because he did what he was told to do? So you also, when

you have done everything you were told to do, should say, "We are unworthy servants; we have only done our duty." (Luke 17:7-10)

And again, Christ set the example at the Last Supper, when He washed the disciples' feet, and commanded His followers to do the same for one another. The reason that we must think in these terms is because no one can truly put the desires of the Lord, or anyone else, before his own, when he is self-centered and thinking only of himself. But if the Christian is to please his Lord, then he must put the desires of God before his own; his tendency towards self-centeredness and putting his own desires first must go.

Thus, contrary to what some today would have us believe, God does not exist solely for the purpose of making man's life better, happier, or more enjoyable; we are to be His servants. Christ didn't die on a cross just to enrich this life for mankind; He died to save the Christian from eternal damnation. And why did He do that? The Scriptures tell us,

> And He died for all, that those who live should no longer live for themselves but for him who died for them and was raised again. (II Corin. 5:15)

Therefore, God's purpose in saving those whom He did save was only that they, in return, should love Him and dedicate their lives to Him for His glory.

Now, it must be obvious at this point that if Christ died for us in order that we might dedicate our lives to His service, it would be a rather despicable practice to claim the salvation He offers and the accompanying benefits without rendering unto Him the service which is rightfully His. But who is honestly shocked to come upon a "self-centered Christian" in our culture? That the church needs to place more emphasis on this teaching is clear, for in this age, even Christians seem to consider it normal to be self-centered. If anyone seriously has doubts about this point, let him closely examine the majority of Christian bookstores and libraries in this land. There may be exceptions, but generally, very few books are stocked dealing with doctrine, holiness, and the nature of God. The best sellers are usually books which deal with the Christian's personal life—topics such as coping with worry and depression, problems with money and family life, and how the church should respond to such things as women's rights, not to mention the huge number of autobiographies. Now, there is nothing wrong with these books in themselves (so long as they come up with the Biblical answer), and indeed, they serve a useful purpose; but the huge emphasis on these matters clearly maps out a trend. This trend indicates that many, if not the majority, of the Christians in this land are not placing as much emphasis on serving God as they are on themselves, and how a relationship with God can benefit them in their personal lives.

But if the Christian is to spend his life in service to the Lord, these matters are really of little importance. For if we truly are putting the desires of Christ before our own, there is no reason for us to be worrying and depressed about our lot in life in the first place. And if we are truly concerned with serving the Most High, what excuse is there for concentrating our thoughts solely on gain of earthly wealth? And many people today certainly do have problems in their family life; but if everyone in that family were totally selfless, and put the desires of Christ and one another before their own, how many divorces would we need? And certainly the least of our problems is whether we should seriously consider the path of the feminists in their zeal to obtain more rights for women in the church—for the whole purpose of the Christian walk is to teach us to give up our "rights," and to learn how to become servants, that we might put others before ourselves.

The true Christian must come to see that the will of Christ is to be the very essence of his life. If we are to be God's servants, how can we place our own desires ahead of the Lord's? That this is inconsistent must be clear to all.

Self-centeredness works in direct opposition to the growth of love, which virtually consists of a zeal to put the desires of God (and one another) before our own. If we are to develop a love for God which will lead to obedience, then our tendencies towards self-centeredness must be eliminated. The Christian must learn to think of himself as a servant of the Most High, indeed, even as a slave; for only then can he take the emphasis off of his own life and place it on God, where it belongs.

If we are to truly please the Lord, or have any true happiness ourselves, it must come by surrendering our wills totally to Christ. His concerns must become our concerns, His goals, our goals, and

His desires, our desires. Therefore, if we must worry at all, let us not waste our time worrying about money, but rather, worrying about the millions of people who have never heard the Gospel, or because we have disobeyed our Lord. If we must be depressed, let us become depressed over the fate of those who have heard the Gospel and rejected it. And if we must concern ourselves with "rights," let us be concerned over the fact that those who place their "rights" above obedience to God will eventually get the equality they deserve—in Hell, where everyone suffers an equally unbearable torture for an equally eternal period.

Our goal as Christians must always be to follow Christ, our Example. The true Christian must concentrate on Him always, putting aside the old nature as best he can, by the power of the Spirit. This, in essence, is the second condition of reform: that we make God the chief authority in our own lives as Christians.

Our Knowledge of God and His Will

Besides developing a right heart towards God, there is another aspect of proper obedience which must be considered: our knowledge of God and His will. For it is clearly impossible for the Christian to obey the Lord when he doesn't even know what He has commanded him to do. No amount of zeal or reverence alone can suffice in leading us to obedience, when we are ignorant of His teachings.

Therefore, both of these conditions, a right heart and a knowledge of God's will, are necessary for the balanced Christian life. If we meet only the second requirement, possessing a knowledge of what God requires, but no motivation to do it, our Christianity becomes only a sterile intellectualism. Much as been said and written about this danger in recent years. But the other extreme, while often ignored, is much more popular today, and may perhaps be the more dangerous of the two. For one of the advantages of a sterile intellectualism is the fact that it is sterile, and hence self-destructive. This other extreme, however, where we possess a zeal for God based on ignorance, seems to be ever popular in this age.

The Christian must strive to avoid either extreme, and give due emphasis to both of these aspects of obedience. The Lord cannot be properly obeyed without either of them.

The danger of placing too little emphasis on a sincere knowledge and acceptance of God's Word cannot be stressed enough. The number of "born-again" Christians today who have only rarely, or perhaps never, read the Bible is a cause for genuine concern, especially in the "experience-oriented" and charismatic churches. The people from such churches are generally eager to tell about how coming to Christ has changed their lives, but the important question is, What are their lives being changed to? The goal of the Christian is to be conformed to the image of Christ—but how can they do this if they do not really know what Christ was like? The end result of this ignorance is a Christian life based on hearsay. Under the influence of this ignorance, it is not uncommon to find some who view the sum total of the Christian life as abstinance from alcohol and tobacco.

A person's actions automatically follow his true inward beliefs. Therefore, if we are to behave like Christians, then we must think like Christians. This knowledge can only be gained, accurately, through an examination of God's Word. The Christian should become so well acquainted with this Book that he comes to really know God, both in his heart and his head. Only then can he truly understand what God's perspective is on the various issues which confront the church today.

The Bible is God's "operating manual" for the Christian life. It is in the Scriptures that God's instructions are revealed most clearly. To go forth with a zeal in life to do God's will, but refusing to take the little time it requires to read His book telling us what to do, is senseless. It is tragic to think that many Christians will spend a whole lifetime doing what they consider to be "God's work," only to discover in the end that it was worthless.

Chapter 6

The Third Condition of Reform: God's Authority in the Collective Church

Certainly one of the major faults in so many present-day plans for church reform is the tendency to ignore social interaction between Christians as a possible means of extending God's authority throughout the Christian society. Most such attempts at regeneration have focused on the Christian's duty to discipline himself only. In Chapter 3, however, it was shown that truly Biblical reform demands that we go beyond this in some cases of gross offense, and that the Christian must often seek to exert discipline on others, also; that is, the unsaved. But as we proceed to examine the Scriptures even further, it becomes clear that God also expects the believer to exert his influence in the lives of other Christians, whenever it is appropriate, for their edification.

It is important that the Christian carefully examine this point and understand it, for Satan has made a valiant attempt in this century to cloud this issue over with all kinds of obstructions—for he certainly knows above all others how strongly God's power is multiplied in the lives of His followers when they are united in fellowship. Surely one of the church's greatest strengths is the mutual love and reinforcement of the Christian society, and Satan will do anything he can to keep God's people from helping one another submit to the Lord.

This social interaction between Christians is clearly an essential part of reform—for who honestly expects every single Christian in the church to fully apply himself toward achieving a state of holiness? Even if the unsaved element were fully removed, the fact remains that the true Christian will often fall into a state of sin; and while God's Spirit works in the lives of all true believers, His presence can sometimes be demonstrated best through others, who are acting in accordance with His will. Therefore, if we are to even partially compensate for the failure of others, necessity demands that we take an active role in the spiritual growth of our fellow Christian.

Surely we can see that this is a practical help in life. For what Christian would not find it easier to obey the Lord when supported by a church motivated towards holiness, than a church which is content with superficial rituals? And is it not even more obvious that a person will find it easier to submit to God's decrees while backed by a church which inflicts discipline and punishment for disobedience, than a church where to obey means to be ridiculed?

Therefore, it must be clear to all that a comprehensive reform of the church cannot be looked upon merely from the aspect of the individual, but necessarily calls for a collective spirit of submission to God. For when this "collective" or "peer pressure" is oriented towards God in the church, as it should be, then even many of the unsaved members will tend to fall in line with God's decrees (in an outward manner)—not because they have a heart right towards Him, but because they are afraid to go against the thought of the majority. And conversely, if this social pressure is allowed to fall into the hands of the wrong men, then the true Christians will literally be persecuted in their own churches—for to insist on obeying God in a congregation where this is an unfashionable practice cannot help but draw scorn from the majority.

The danger here lies in the fact that man is strongly encouraged or discouraged to do certain things, depending upon the views of those about him. This danger is indeed very real, and makes it of the utmost importance that Christians use this matter of social interaction and reinforcement to their advantage. For if we do not, we can rest assured that Satan will not hesitate to use it against us.

The Third Condition of Reform

This third condition of reform, then, must deal with the means by which the Christian can exert his influence in the life of other believers for the purpose of edification. Since man is strongly influenced by the opinions of those about him, and is quite often rather lax in disciplining himself, Christians must seek to provide support for one another. And while even this may not result in a foolproof scheme, this will bring us as close to a state of reform as is possible, working with imperfect humans and the conditions that we presently face; for what more can be done than to remove the rebellious, and to work towards perfection, through the power of God's Spirit, both in ourselves and in our fellow Christian? Our goal in reform is to bring the entire church into submission to the authority of God, and we must do everything within our power to assist others in the Faith submit to that Authority.

In order to determine the proper way to do this, the Christian must first look to the Scriptures and note what guidance God has given us in this matter. It was demonstrated earlier that the key to the Christian's relationship with God was found in the first and greatest commandment—that is, the love for God which follows as a natural result of the salvation purchased by Christ. This would cause the true believer to willingly submit to His decrees. But is there a similar rule to guide the Christian in his relationships with other believers?

We find such a rule in Matthew 22:34-40, which says:

> Hearing that Jesus had silenced the Sadducees, the Pharisees got together. One of them, an expert in the law, tested him with this question: "Teacher, which is the greatest commandment in the Law?"
>
> Jesus replied: "Love the Lord your God with all your heart and with all your soul and with all your mind." This is the first and greatest commandment. And the second is like it: "Love your neighbor as yourself." All the Law and the Prophets hang on these two commandments (NIV).

Thus, we find that just as the Christian's love for God covers the first table of the law, our love for one another covers the second; indeed, obedience to these two commandments fulfills the whole law. But just what does it mean here to "love your neighbor?" And perhaps more specifically, just how do we love our brethren in the church?

We find the answer to this in I John 5:2,3, which says: "This is how we know that we love the children of God: by loving God and carrying out his commands. This is love for God: to obey his commands" (NIV). Hence, the Christian shows love for others in the same way that he shows love for God: by obeying His commandments. In this case, of course, we are referring primarily to the second table of the Law, and all of the implications included therein. Thus, a man shows love for his neighbor by not stealing from him, lying about him, murdering him, or committing adultery with his wife. In short, we love our neighbor by obeying God's Law with respect to him, and doing nothing that will harm him (Romans 13:9,10).

Now, this statement must be taken with a certain degree of latitude, in that the Law, by necessity, is somewhat general in nature. For instance, Jesus gives us the parable of the Good Samaritan as an example of what it means to love our neighbor. But no where does the Law specifically say, "If you happen to come upon a man who has been beaten and robbed, you must bandage his wounds, put him on your donkey, take him to the nearest inn, give the innkeeper some money, and promise to cover the remainder of the expenses when you come by later." Clearly, this parable is included in more general commands, such as Matthew 23:23, Matthew 5:7, and Deuteronomy 22:4, concerning mercy and helping one another. When we state that love is shown through obedience to the law, we do not mean that obedience in an outward way to the very letter is acceptable even if the heart is wrong, or that we can safely ignore any need not specifically written in the law; only that the Christian must not depend upon his "feelings" to dictate what love is or is not. Generally, we will not go far wrong in performing acts of kindness; but if the Scriptures do not clearly spell out a point, the Christian need only ask himself whether such an action would bring glory to God, or in any way encourage rebellion against Him. This must always be the deciding factor.

Now, it is clear that the number of ways in which love can be shown to another are virtually endless. It would therefore be pointless to attempt to examine every single aspect of this subject. But with reference to this topic of reform in the church, it is important that we consider just what it means to love our neighbor with respect to his growth in the Lord. For since it is every man's chief duty in life to know and glorify God, what greater act of love can we render a brother than assisting him in this goal? Certainly, this matter should take precedence over any material benefits, as eternal life is of much greater value than worldly gains. Therefore, if the Christian truly desires to demonstrate love for his brother, the most beneficial means of doing so is to aid him in developing a strong relationship with the Lord.

We can see this principle clearly displayed in the life of Christ. In John 15:12, 13, He says, "My command is this: Love each other as I have loved you. Greater love has no one than this, that one lay down his life for his friends" (NIV). The thing to note here is not only the tendency to put the welfare of others ahead of His own, as important as that is, but also the reason this supreme sacrifice was made. Was it to bring comfort, peace, a life of ease, or material wealth to His followers? Obviously not, for the "rewards" most of His disciples received were torture, persecution, and execution. This supreme sacrifice was not made to make the earthly life of His followers more enjoyable, as such, but to reconcile them with God. Furthermore, even though Jesus performed many acts of healing, and did do numerous things to help people in this life, it is clear from Scripture that His primary intent was always to draw these people closer to the Father.

Therefore, as His disciple, the Christian must seek to follow His example. Helping others in Christ with their worldly needs is both desirable and necessary, but concern for their spiritual growth is even better.

Now, this assistance which the Christian can offer can take on two basic forms: a "positive" form of assistance, where the goal is primarily to encourage and uphold one another in the Faith, and a "disciplinary" approach, which consists mainly of admonishments and rebukes given when necessary to restore or correct. Both of these approaches have their necessary roles in the life of the church.

As far as the process of reform is concerned, the first approach serves largely in the role of what might be called "preventive medicine." By praying with and for one another, meeting together collectively for worship, performing acts of charity, and providing other such means of spiritual reinforcement, the Christian helps and upholds his brother. There can be no doubt that these positive means of spiritual reinforcement are essential to the well-being of the church.

The second form consists primarily of admonishments and rebukes given to one another, when necessary, to prevent them from giving in to, or repeating, a tendency towards sin. (By "sin," we are not necessarily referring to every sin that is committed, for even most Christians, if not all, sin daily in some respect—if not in deed, at least in thought. We are concerned here with a sinful tendency occuring repeatedly, gross sins, or any sin which the Christian may seem complacent about, not every "slip" that is committed and then repented of.) The value of giving such rebukes to a brother when he sins or is in backsliding can hardly be overestimated. Every Christian has tendencies towards spiritual sluggishness at times, and when he finds himself becoming complacent or apathetic, nothing spurs a person on like a rebuke. Nor will anything tend to keep him from sin so much as knowing that to do so will draw down reproach from his closest acquaintances. A rebuke is even more important when given publicly to offset a public sin; in such cases, the embarrassment to the offender will not only cause him to refrain from repeating such action, but also serves as an example to the rest of the congregation, that they also might not commit his error.

Thus, in his first letter to Timothy, Paul tells him, "Those who sin are to be rebuked publicly, so that the others may take warning" (I Tim. 5:20) (NIV), and to Titus he wrote, "Therefore, rebuke them sharply, so that they will be sound in the faith" (Titus 1:13) (NIV), concerning those who sought to lead the people astray. And as the Proverb teaches, "A rebuke impresses a man of discernment more than a hundred lashes a fool" (Prov. 17:10) (NIV), and again, "Whoever loves discipline loves knowledge, but he who hates correction is stupid" (Prov. 12:1) (NIV). Certainly the power built into such a plan is obvious. For one of the things which no doubt makes it so tempting to sin in the first place is the fact that God is invisible to our eyes, and hence, His presence seems somewhat less real to us. But would any Christian enter into sin so lightly if Jesus, in human form, were staring over his shoulder? Likewise, other Christians in the church, and especially the church authorities, can serve as His representatives to promote the same effect.

At least in principle, most Christians today would have no complaints about the first approach, even if they do not always consistently practice it, but this disciplinary approach has been allowed to fall into disrepute. It is interesting to note the parallels here between the average Christian's response to the presence of the unsaved in the church and to the presence of sin in his fellow believer. In both cases, the modern Christian often seems to consider it his duty to overlook the offense—and for the same reason: that he is required to "love" his brother, and is therefore prohibited from making judgments about him, let alone punishing him. This modern concept of love refuses to admit that love can be expressed in any disciplinary form. Hence, evil is allowed to go unchecked in its desire to destroy God's church.

The Christian must always remember that true love consists

of obeying God, in both his relationships with the Lord and with one another. This means that since God has commanded Christians to look after one another and admonish each other when called for (Gal. 6:1,2), then to do this is an expression of love. To attempt to avoid obedience for the sake of politeness, or in order to avoid hurting someone's feelings, is not only sinful, but in a very real sense, a display of hate, or at the very least, negligence.

Consider, for instance, the Golden Rule. Jesus tells us that to do unto others as we would have them do unto us is the sum of the Law; that is, love (Matthew 7:12; Romans 13:8). But what happens when this rule is applied to a case of discipline, such as with a disobedient child? No normal child would want to be spanked—does this mean then that love is expressed by holding back discipline, since we would not want the discipline if we were in the child's place?

Of course not. Indeed, God says that any man who holds back the rod from his son hates him (Proverbs 13:24). What we must understand is that when we are instructed to do unto others as we would have them do unto us, God is not commanding us to deal with them according to their own preferences, or the preferences of our pleasure-seeking society. Rather, He is telling us to do unto others what is right and good, and to their best advantage. This is how we are to deal with Christian brothers who fall into sin. We must chastise them if we love them.

If the Christian truly wishes to love his brother, and to reform the church, then he must not hold back discipline. When a brother sins, he should not hesitate to show him his error, if need be. Neither should be recoil from being chastised himself when he is corrected for having committed a wrong. For no enemy of man can be worse than sin, which separates us from God; hence, anyone who seeks to save us from it is a true friend indeed. Only a most sickly form of "love" would advise us to turn our backs on another Christian in a moment of spiritual weakness.

The Christian must remember, however, that the sanctification of a brother, like that of himself, is a process essentially under the control of God and given by grace. The only direct influence we can truly have is through prayer, since it is God's Spirit alone who can truly have an effect on men's hearts. These outward actions are necessary, and God does work through them, but in any attempt to discipline ourselves or others, we must remember this and pray first, that God might use these efforts for His glory and to achieve whatever end He has appointed.

Now, if these rebukes and other forms of discipline are indeed all that essential to the well-being of the church, why is it that this practice is currently under such heavy attack? Not only do most churches or Christians not practice this, but in all likelihood, would judge such action to be inappropriate. What is responsible for this strange rejection of discipline? What force at work in our society would encourage the Christian to think of discipline as evil, and insist that complacency and tolerance of evil are "love"? Since this discipline is one of the chief means by which God's authority is made present in the church, it is clear that we must seek out and destroy that which is preventing this practice from prospering.

Moral Judgments are Part of the Christian Life

In Chapter 3, it was necessary to refute two erroneous patterns of thought common in modern Western society: not only the concept that love is relativistic—that is, can be defined individually—but also the notion that we are forbidden to make any judgments about one another. Both of these concepts derive their origin not from Christianity, but from humanism, which has saturated Western culture for some time with its poisonous teachings. Clearly, if these Biblical principles of social discipline are to be restored to their rightful place in the church, then we must first rid it of these humanistic and relativistic heresies. These heresies teach that there is no absolute right and wrong, and that the Christian must therefore turn his head the other way when a brother sins, and allow the offender to decide for himself whether his action is right, independently of God's Law. This, of course, works directly in opposition to the principles of reform just set forth; therefore, we must examine these points further, that the reader might note the parallels involved in the mechanisms responsible for hindering both this and the first condition of reform.

To begin with, both the first condition of reform and this third condition require that the Christian be willing to make moral judgments concerning his brethren in the church, and willing to take action under the proper circumstances. Now, it is certain that the second condition will meet with much less opposition, as it requires only that the person look within himself. This idea modern thought is willing to tolerate, which is probably why nearly all current writers on this subject have laid all of the emphasis on self-discipline only. But this idea that we must hold others accountable for their actions, and that we ourselves must be held accountable in the eyes of our peers, is met to a large degree only with intolerance. Indeed, in some relativistic patterns of thought, where it is consistently held that no absolute right or wrong exists, it would seem that the only "wrong" one could commit would be to accuse someone else of having committed a wrong!

This reluctance of our society to hold others accountable for their actions clearly stems from the growth of humanism in our culture. Since humanism places the desires of men before the authority of God, and is centered around men instead of God, it must, by necessity, have a relativistic base. This, in turn, makes it extremely vulnerable to criticism, for if any of its basic teachings are brought into question, it has no true authority to which it can appeal for support. Therefore, with nothing on which to base their doctrine, their only recourse to avoid refutation, or at least charges of superficiality, is to force a perverted interpretation of Scripture verses such as Matthew 7:1 on the church, so as to avoid judgment altogether, lest they be judged, and found wanting.

Hence, in order to escape from those who would openly display his error, the humanist must resort to such lines as these: "Who are you to judge?" or "What gives you the right to judge me?" The motive of these people, clearly, is not an ardent zeal for obedience to Matthew 7:1, but rather, is an attempt to escape moral accountability altogether. The humanist mind must invariably appeal to such slogans; since his system is based not on a true authority but on the mere whims of man, attempting to escape criticism altogether is his only defense.

To say that someone else's sins are not any of the church's business is shallow minded; for when a person enters the church, he makes it everyone's business. To stay outside and bring disgrace on himself in his business—but to enter the church as a Christian and bring disgrace on the Lord is the whole church's business.

Realizing then, that this tendency to avoid making moral judgments is derived from a system anti-Christian in nature, it becomes clear that the Christian's duty is to ignore such teachings and cling to the advice of Scripture. This advice also includes, of course, the fact that we are not to judge others with wrong motives or on an improper authority; we are not nullifying the command given in Matt. 7:1, which is indeed valid. Neither are we to pronounce judgment on those outside the church (I Corin. 5). The Christian must not go beyond what he is commanded, but he must not make the opposite mistake and ignore his duty altogether, either. Our duty is to love one another, and when true love requires that we discipline one another, we must do just that. Determining when the situation is "proper" may not always be easy; in these cases, we should only proceed after much prayer in the matter. But the goal before us in this is edification—the deciding factor must always be whether our actions would bring restoration, or hinder it.

When confronting those in the church who have been heavily influenced by this humanistic thought, probably the best way to deal with this problem is simply to counsel and admonish them when their erroneous pattern of thought leads them down the wrong path. If their response is to come up with some puerile line such as, "Who are you to judge?" they should be rebuked, and made to understand that the motive is to help, not to criticize, and that you therefore do have the right to confront them. If they remain obstinate, they are more than likely unregenerate, and should be dealt with according to the principles set forth in Chapter 4.

The Role of Secondary Authorities in the Church

Up until this point in the discussion of this chapter, it has largely been assumed that all believers are on equal levels of authority within the church, and we have therefore covered this matter of social discipline in somewhat of a general way. But a little thought on this matter will quickly reveal the inadequacy of such a position. For one thing, the average layman in the church can inflict only a rather limited degree of discipline on any particular offender; other than an admonishment or a rebuke, he can do very little. Hence, the need exists for a human authority to deal with the more difficult cases. Secondly, human leadership is needed in Christian relationships to maintain order and provide direction among the church as a whole.

The existence of such human authorities is clearly essential, for if man's chief end is to know and glorify God, then any family, church, or other social group can only rightly have this same end in view. But in order for this to be achieved as a collective effort, the individuals composing that group must all be thinking in terms of a common goal. And while human leadership might not be necessary in all cases, the Scriptures speaking as plainly as they do, it is nevertheless important that we have them when we do need them. Hence, we see that God has provided His church with such leaders in both the Old and New Testament times, to maintain this unity of thought, and to enforce the obedience necessary to achieve the desired ends.

The relative importance of these secondary authorities can perhaps be seen more clearly by comparing the church to an army (which is not at all an unfitting analogy, as the church is indeed at war with the powers of darkness, and the Christian is referred to in the Scriptures as a "soldier"—Eph. 6:11-18; 2 Tim. 2:3). Consider for a moment the utter confusion and chaos which would result if all of the officers were removed from a large army, and each man was allowed to follow his own favorite battle plan. Obviously, such a scheme would be unworkable and useless; that each and every man might indeed be in loyal submission to the Commander-in-Chief does not change the fact in the least that secondary authorities are needed. Likewise, God has chosen to delegate His authority in this manner, both in the home and in the church, in order to give these social institutions stability and to maintain an orderly pattern of living and worship. (God also delegates authority to government, but the effects of this on the reform of the church are indirect; we will therefore confine our discussion to the church and the home).

God has so designed the church and home that their existence and well-being are highly dependent upon maintaining these positions of authority. When they are ignored or abandoned, then rebellion and spiritual chaos are the only possible results. It is therefore of the utmost importance that we understand the necessity of these authorities, and do everything within our power to uphold them in both integrity and honor.

The purpose for which God has appointed these secondary authorities is that they might lead the church to know and glorify Him as a collective whole. This helps to compensate for those who are still weak in the Faith or ignorant of Biblical principles. Thus, since these men are given positions of such authority by God, to rebel against them unjustly is essentially the same as rebelling against God Himself. God has appointed these men to maintain an orderly system of worship and living which will glorify Himself; so long as they are doing this, anyone who rejects their authority is disrupting the church and is in defiance of God's authority. We can see, then, that this matter of submission to secondary authorities is of crucial importance not only in reforming the church, but even in living the Christian life, period. Because this is such an important part of maintaining God's authority in the Christian society, and because the attitude of our society towards this matter is currently rather lax, let us look into this more closely.

The Relationship Between Authoritative Superiors and Inferiors in the Christian Society

The number of Scripture verses pertaining to this matter is rather large, no doubt due to the importance of such instruction. Some of them, such as in Ephesians 5 and I Timothy 2, dealing with the submission of women to their husbands and in the church, are relatively well-known due to their controversial nature in a humanistic society. Others, on the other hand, are virtually ignored. But a general summary of all these points is conveniently laid out for us in the *Larger Catechism of the Westminster Standards*, which have long been recognized by virtually all Christendom as one of, if not the, best and most accurate statements of doctrine ever written for the church. Every statement in the text is substantiated by Scripture, proofs of which are given following the answers, to reinforce its trustworthiness.

Turning now to this catechism, we find the following statements:

> (Question 129) "What is required of superiors towards their inferiors?" Reply: "It is required of superiors, according to that power they receive from God, and that relation wherein they stand, to love, pray for, and bless their inferiors, to instruct, counsel and admonish them, countenancing, commending, and rewarding such as do well, and discountenancing, reproving, and chastising such as do ill; protecting, and providing for them all things

necessary for soul and body; and by grave, wise, holy, and exemplary carriage, to procure glory to God, and honour to themselves, and so to preserve that authority which God hath put upon them."

And again, Question 130 reads,

"What are the sins of superiors?" Reply: "The sins of superiors are, besides the neglect of the duties required of them, an inordinate seeking of themselves, their own glory, ease, profit, or pleasure, commanding things unlawful, or not in the power of inferiors to perform, counselling, encouraging, or favouring them in that which is evil; dissuading, discouraging, or discountenancing them in that which is good, correcting them unduly, careless exposing, or leaving them to wrong, temptation, and danger; provoking them to wrath, or any way dishonoring themselves, or lessening their authority, by an unjust, indiscreet, rigorous, or remiss behavior."

(The terms "superior" and "inferior," as they are used here, refer only to the relative authoritative rank. In the army, for instance, a captain is a "superior" to a private; but this does not imply that the captain is of any more worth as a man, in general. Likewise, these terms do not mean here that a superior is necessarily any better or of any greater importance—only that God has assigned to him a higher station of authority.)

Certainly these men have given the Christian an accurate, concise, and Biblical account here of his duties towards his authoritative inferiors. But for our purposes these passages can be summarized more briefly still. In the first reply, the duty first set forth is for the superior to love those placed under him. This is, of course, perfectly reasonable—for if he loves them, he will not want to violate any of the other duties after that. Indeed, the remainder of the list is merely an elaboration of the various ways in which he shows his love towards them:

(1) he prays for them and blesses them,
(2) he instructs them in the teachings of Scripture —rewarding them if they do well, and reproving them if they do not;

(3) he provides for their spiritual and material needs; and
(4) he lives an exemplary life before them, both to set a good example, and to preserve the authority which God has entrusted to him.

Likewise, the second reply could well be summarized as a state wherein the superior puts his own interests ahead of those who have been placed under him, or at least does not care enough for them:

(1) he is not to possess an inordinate seeking of himself;
(2) he is not to encourage or command anything wrong or unlawful—nor to discourage anything good;
(3) he is not to reprove them too harshly or for something which is not evil; and
(4) he is not to commit actions himself which would tend to set a bad example and lessen his authority.

Although there may be other factors which a good Christian leader should consider, we find here the Biblical points which are basic to this position. It is the duty of a Christian with authority over others to love them, and that love is expressed through prayers and blessings, through teaching them God's Word, providing for their needs, and by setting a good example for them. No Christian in authority can consider his duties fulfilled unless he is performing all of these actions.

These general guidelines apply to all who hold authoritative positions: to elders with respect to their congregation, to a man with respect to his wife, and to parents with respect to their children. It is difficult to be anymore specific here, as there are always a great number of variables involved. Indeed, the Scriptures also fail to elaborate further on specifics; let us therefore stop at this point, and state simply that it is the duty of each Christian superior to apply these principles in his own circumstances as the Holy Spirit leads him. Each man with authority over others should keep in mind, however, that his position is a serious one; those who handle this responsibility lightly are warned by Scripture that their punishment will be severe.

Turning now to the duties of inferiors towards those placed over them, we find the following:

Question #127 of the Catechism reads: "What is the honour that inferiors owe to their superiors?" The reply is, "The honour which inferiors owe to their superiors is, all due reverence in heart, word, and behavior, prayer and thanksgiving for them; imitation of their virtues and graces; willing obedience to their lawful commands and counsels; due submission to their corrections; fidelity to, defence, and maintenance of their persons and authority, according to their several ranks, and the nature of their places; bearing with their infirmities, and covering them in love, that so they may be an honour to them and to their government."

And to the following question, "What are the sins of inferiors against their superiors?" we find the following reply:

"The sins of inferiors against their superiors are, all neglect of their duties required towards them; envying at, comtempt of, and rebellion against their persons and places, in their lawful counsels, commands, and corrections; cursing, mocking, and all such refractory and scandalous carriage, as proves a shame and dishonour to them and their government."

Once again, we can, for our purposes, summarily state these points as follows:

Inferiors have the following duties towards their superiors:
(1) they must reverence them in all things,
(2) they must pray for their superiors;
(3) they must seek to learn from and imitate their virtues and graces,
(4) they must be willing to obey their lawful commandments, and submit to correction when they fail; and
(5) They must remain loyal and submissive to their persons and positions of authority, covering them in love, despite their many imperfections.

The sins of inferiors include the following:
(1) neglecting any of the above duties;

(2) envy at, contempt of, or rebellion against the superior's authority, in any case where the command, counsel, or correction was lawful, and
(3) any attempt to dishonor or lower the status of those placed over them.

As clear and explicit as these statements are, and considering also the strong Biblical backing for them, one would think that this should be the end of the matter. However, as in the case of the superiors, we too often find these duties neglected in the church today, particularly in these areas:

(1) The first area in which we find trouble involves those in positions of lower authority attempting to seize a higher position than to which they have been assigned by God. Here, we are not referring exclusively to the more radical cases, such as appointing women or even children to positions of authority in the church, as some denominations have done, but even to the fact that many "qualified" men in the ministry and eldership have not truly been called to that position. Even if a man meets all of the external requirements (Titus 1:6-9 and I Tim. 3:1-7), he should not attempt to take a position unless it is clear that he is called to that position by God.
(2) The second area in which we currently find trouble is in those who do not strictly attempt to attain power themselves, but instead try to whittle down the authority of those above them in order to establish an "equality." This is more common in husband-wife relationships.

The problem with both of these kinds of thought is that they are motivated by human pride. It is difficult for some men to understand why they have not been appointed to a position of authority in the church, or to the ministry; they somehow feel that they would make a more capable leader than the one whom God has chosen. And some women may find it hard to understand why they are required by God to obey their husbands, or are banned from the church leadership altogether. Human pride cries out to these people that this is unjust; they are sure that they could handle that position just as well as anyone else.

All such thinking, however, only serves to prove them wrong. For if they were indeed suitable for any position of spiritual leadership, they would not be thinking in such ways to begin with. For this line of thought is invariably rooted in a desire to be the master, rather than a servant. We are envious and proud, and tend to think of ourselves as being too important to accept a lower status. The Christian should keep in mind, however, that Satan was cast out of Heaven for this very crime—he, too, was proud, and wanted to be the Master, not the servant (Isaiah 14:12-15); as a result, he is now the father of all those who follow in this path.

The true Christian is not to think in this way. The Scriptures constantly remind him to think of himself as a servant, and to be humble in spirit. He is not, as the disciples did in Mark 9:33, 34, to argue over who is the greatest or most important. Christians are to think of themselves as one another's servants, and put the desires of others ahead of their own.

Those who relentlessly clamor for their "rights" can never be strong Christians, and it is unlikely that they are Christians at all, because they are motivated by forces which work in direct opposition to the Christian life. Those who are worried about such things are invariably puffed up with pride, think too highly of themselves, and are more interested in what they can take rather than give. How can anyone be honestly learning to think of himself as a servant, and at the same time protest because he feels he is entitled to a higher position? Surely this inconsistency must be apparent to all.

Because of the rapid growth of humanism in our culture, which thrives on human pride, many churches and Christians have lost their perspective on this matter. The church needs to place more emphasis on the necessity of obedience to these secondary authorities, and the pattern of thought the Christian himself should maintain. We must constantly stress in our services that those who would be the head in God's Kingdom must be the servant of all, and that the position of a servant is highly esteemed in God's eyes.

Obviously, our society does not think this way; indeed, it thinks exactly the opposite, and so do many persons currently in the churches. This is probably nowhere displayed more clearly than in the attempts of some women to gain positions in the ministry.

They often try to excuse such action by stating that Paul, or some other apostle, was culturally influenced in his writings (which, of course, cannot be true, for the Holy Spirit has inspired these passages—if Paul was "culturally deceived," then so was God). Then they often state that what he wrote may have been true at that time, but is no longer true due to changes in our culture and standards (This argument is equally hopeless, for God's decrees have never been based on any culture, but on His own nature and preferences. Paul also specifically states that these particular commandments which he gave were not based on his culture, but on creational principles (I Tim. 2:13, 14)). But the interesting thing to note here is the attitude of these people. It is clear that their thoughts are not really directed towards how they can please God the most, but rather, how they can make their own preferences seem acceptable in spite of what God has stated. For even these people must admit that their interpretation concerning Scripture is at least questionable; so, if they truly wished to please God, and there is even a chance that what they are doing might offend Him, why do it?

There is obviously only one reasonable answer: they are putting their own pride and interests ahead of the Lord. They consider a state of submission to be degrading, and their pride motivates them to go for something "better." If anyone seriously questions this, let him examine for himself the writings given in defense of this practice—how often is the desire to please God and the need to submit to His authority stressed? The dead giveway is when some writers attempt to justify this by stating that the "curse of Genesis 3," inflicted as a result of Eve's actions, was removed by Christ's first coming (why this should be so is rather obscure; the curse against the man and serpent, as well as death, are still in force). The interesting thing to note here is that these people invariably think that the punishment that God inflicted on the woman was that she would have to live in submission to her husband. But this is not true; the Bible states that the woman was created for the man from the very beginning. Likewise, Paul tells us in Ephesians 5 that the relationship between a man and his wife is symbolic of the relationship between Christ and His church—that the man should love his wife with a self-giving love, and that the wife should respect her husband and submit to him. But note that this was just as true before the fall into sin in Eden as it was afterwards. Thus, the woman's duty to submit to her husband began in creation, not when they fell into sin. When God therefore states in Genesis 3:16 that the woman's punishment was that her husband would rule over her, this does not mean that submission is the punishment; for this was her duty all along. The real "curse of Genesis 3" is that the man to whom the woman must submit would now be a sinner, a being who would not always love her as he should, and would oftentimes degrade her and treat her very cruelly.

The point of all this is that the sinful nature in man does indeed think of being in submission to another person as a "curse." Our society tends to regard such submission to an authority as degrading, and beneath a person's dignity. The old nature, whether the remnant that still exists within the Christian, or more commonly, under full control in the unregenerate, constantly tells man to insist on his own way, that it is better to be on top, to take rather than give, and that we should do whatever will please us the most. Lost men always seek these things.

But the Christian should not think this way. He must not think of submission to an authority placed over him as degrading or beneath his dignity. They have been placed over us by God for our own good. Regardless, humble submission is a quality highly praised in Scripture, and such an attitude is listed as essential to the Christian life (Mark 10:42-45).

The Christian must be careful not to seek to overthrow that authority which God has placed over him for his own good. The Biblical concept of submission to a head is not very popular today—if it ever was—and the vast inroads which worldliness and humanism have made in some churches in this century has certainly made matters worse. But God has nevertheless commanded all Christians to be in subjection to those whom He has ordained as their superiors, and are therefore guilty of no small sin when they refuse them that submission.

Hence, when the Christian is placed in a situation such as this, he must not rebel against the lawful and correct requests of his superiors. Some men may feel that they are better qualified for the job than those whom God has appointed; and some women may feel that they are perfectly capable of leadership positions. And these statements may indeed be true, when viewed from a human perspective. The leaders in the churches are not always the strongest, and there may be many very capable women who could fulfill these earthly duties. But that has absolutely nothing to do with it; for God is not concerned with human strength or ability—but in obedience, and in furthering His own glory through whatever means He appoints. And often, He deliberately chooses human weakness as a means of demonstrating His power.

God has created everyone for a certain purpose, and everyone has an appointed role to fill in this life. Therefore, we are not to rashly seize upon someone else's position because we think it is more beneficial or important, but should remain content with whatever lot God has assigned to us in life. If God has called us to be a missionary, then we should be a missionary. If God has called us to be a housewife, then we should be a housewife. If God has called us to be a garbageman, then we should be a garbageman. Anyone who uses the talents God gave him in the manner that God has appointed, and for His glory, will receive their full reward. For all of these abilities are given by God in the first place; hence, the person involved doesn't deserve any of the credit for whatever success may result. There is no reason then for us to seek the more "important" positions, or try to attain to a higher position of authority than the one we have been assigned to, because the only ones who will receive their reward on Judgment Day are those who faithfully manned their own post, not someone else's.

There are, of course, some cases where disobedience to a human authority is necessary and good. The main justification for this is a situation where obedience to the human authority will result in disobedience to God, or authorities exist who are in defiance of God by accepting that position. Indeed, there may be times when the Christian finds it necessary to have a particular leader removed from his position altogether. It is especially important that churches in corrupt denominations not allow themselves to be railroaded into accepting a leadership that is in defiance of God's Word. If this has already happened, such leadership should be removed, if possible. But such rebellion should never be practiced unless there can be no doubt that it is required by God's Word.

This is indeed a problem today, though. Many churches not only are tolerant of poor leaders, but even tolerate unsaved men in the elder and minister positions. The Christian must realize that this, too, is an act of rebellion against God, when we allow men to tear down His church without at least trying to stop them.

But other than in a situation such as this, submission to the authorities is mandatory. These authorities have been appointed by God to maintain the order and purity of His church, and to provide an atmosphere wherein each Christian can grow and mature. Those who disrupt the church by fighting such authorities without a valid reason, or attempt to take positions of authority in defiance of the Word, are not only thoughtless, but stand in contempt of the authority of God.

Chapter 7

Conclusions

The three conditions of reform set forth here point out the areas in which the reformer should attempt to concentrate his efforts. The goal of these three conditions, clearly, is to direct the church into a state of submission and obedience to the Lord. No true reformation of any magnitude can take place without due consideration of these factors, because failure to comply with any of them encourages, or at least fails to discourage, disobedience within some segment of the church membership. All truly great reformations of the past have included both a separation from the ungodly and a call to higher discipline on the part of the true believer. (Persecution has often been the motivating factor.)

There are, of course, numerous other factors which enter into the building of a strong church; evangelism, for instance, is an important ingredient. But all of these other factors are merely the "fruits" of an effective reform movement, not a cause of reform; that is, they stem from a proper authoritative relationship with God. This matter of authority is clearly the central issue here; for if we establish a system where God's authority is held in due reverence, then obedience to His commands to evangelize, or to do anything else, will be followed automatically. Likewise, the degree to which we depart from such reverence, the more our minds tend to detract from the importance of proper submission in anything. Therefore, these other factors are really of very little concern at this point, for they are not causes of reform, but merely effects generated by true submission.

Since this matter of authority is central to the issue, the reformer must keep in mind that anyone or anything that attempts to lessen the authority of God is the church's greatest enemy. Of this we can be sure, not only because of the proofs already presented, but also by example and experience. After all, what was the crime of Satan which resulted in his expulsion from Heaven? Isaiah 14 tells us that he became proud, and tried to put himself on a level of authority equal to or greater than that of God. Furthermore, his intent ever since has been to lead all of God's other creatures into rebellion against His authority. It is therefore clear then that to work in direct opposition to Satan, or to be in compliance with God, involves before anything else a willingness to submit to His authority.

The means by which Satan has attempted to generate this rebellion has varied throughout the ages, but his goal is always the same. Therefore, the goal of the reformer never really changes, either. Just as Satan is always seeking to lead others away from obedience to the authority of God, the reformer must seek to lead them to such obedience. This, in itself, is not difficult to grasp; the main problem is that Satan does use different methods in different times to accomplish his ends, and invariably searches for any "blind spots" which that particular church or culture might possess. And since the reformer is often a part of that culture himself, he must be extremely careful that his spiritual evaluations are always based firmly on Scripture.

While the conditions of reform set forth here would apply really to any age, in this book we have sought to place emphasis on how they apply in this time and culture. In contemporary society, one of the greatest hindrances to the start of a reform movement seems to be the presence of much humanistic thought in the church. We must understand, of course, that Satan has always attempted to encourage self-centeredness; the concept that man is his own master, and has the right to do anything he wants, is always appealing to the natural mind. But the danger of this particular type of thought is that it not only seeks to excuse the person of any responsibility towards his sin, but the relativism which must invariably accompany this concept seeks the destruction of discipline and moral accountability altogether.

The foundations of Christianity and secular humanism are, of course, antithetical. But a modified form of humanism has engulfed some churches. Many Christians do not seem to realize that they were created for God purposes, and not the reverse. Their main emphasis is always on what God can do for them, and how becoming a Christian will be of benefit. (The Christian should, of course, be deeply thankful for the benefits God has given him—especially salvation. But he should not be of the delusion that God exists solely for the purpose of making his life more "meaningful.") Worse yet, many Christians have fallen prey to the idea that it is wrong for them to make any moral judgments in life, especially concerning someone else. This is in spite of the fact that the Bible from beginning to end praises those who take action to restrain others from sin.

This type of thought must be removed from the church. Whether it results in us tolerating sin within either ourselves or others, it is dangerous. Like Phinehas in Numbers 25, those who wish to please the Lord must learn to hate evil. The true Christian must always think in terms of his duty and responsibility to God, and not, as his self-centered humanist counterpart, in terms of his own pleasures, desires, and "rights."

At this point, the reader might be curious as to just how serious this problem really has become. Have we blown things out of proportion? Or is the situation actually all that critical?

A brief look at current events is all that is required to answer these questions. We have only to look about us to see what is happening; the degeneration of some church organizations has become so bad that they no longer even attempt to hide their actions. It no longer shocks anyone, for instance, to hear of the World Council of Churches, and the affiliated denominations, giving money to Marxist, revolutionary forces in Africa. Despite the fact that these forces are often involved in terrorist activity, these church groups view it as a necessary expenditure to help "combat racism."[1] Many church related organizations have become dominated by radicals whose main desire seems to be the destruction of capitalism, in order that some form of socialist state may be realized. Hiding under the cover of the church gives them the advantages of tax exemption, access to a large organizational network, and perhaps most important of all, an image of respectability. The activities of these groups can range from outright support and applause of Communist governments to more subtle attacks on the free enterprise system. And while the motivation of some groups may not be quite so sinister, we must at least wonder whether they have perhaps a warped sense of priorities in this respect. Consider, for instance, the recent boycott of the Nestle corporation by the National Council of Churches, for having committed the horrible crime of selling and marketing infant formula in "Third-World" countries.[2] Even if it were possible to produce reliable evidence that this was to some extent justified, is this really the most pressing need the church is confronted with today?

If it sounds as though the priorities of these groups are questionable, they are certainly not alone; the churches themselves often actively support these causes, and some that are worse. How can we help but question the integrity of an organization like the United Church of Christ, when their attempts to fight "racism" include spending over $500,000 in legal expenses to free the "Wilmington 10"—ten persons convicted of fire-bombing during a racial riot, and for shooting at the police and firemen when they came to put the fire out?[3] How can we overlook the many inconsistencies forced on us by the humanistic thought which has engulfed the United Methodist Church? One good example of this can be found in their own *Book of Discipline of the United Methodist Church*. In this work, they first inform us of the fact that "United Methodists share with all other Christians the conviction that Scripture is the primary source and guideline for doctrine."[4] Then they proceed to show us many clear examples of such conviction:

The Scriptures: I tell you that anyone who divorces his wife, except for marital unfaithfulness, and marries another woman commits adultery. (Matthew 19:9) (NIV)
The United Methodists: When marriage partners, even after thoughtful consideration and counsel, are estranged beyond reconciliation, we recognize divorce as regrettable but recognize the right of the divorced persons to remarry.[5]
The Scriptures: Whoever sheds the blood of man, by man shall his blood be shed; for in the image of God has God made man. (Gen. 9:6) (NIV)
Do not accept a ransom for the life of a murderer, who deserves to die. He must surely be put to death. (Numbers 35:31)(NIV)
The United Methodists: In the love of Christ who came to save those who are lost and vulnerable, we urge the creation of genuinely new systems of rehabilitation that will restore, preserve, and nurture the humanity of the imprisoned. For the same reason, we oppose capital punishment and urge its elimination from all criminal codes.[6]
(God did not implement capital punishment because He was incapable of thinking up a means of rehabilitation, but because His just nature can settle for nothing less.)
The Scriptures: I do not permit a woman to teach or to have authority over a man; she must be silent. (I Tim. 2:12) (NIV)

As in all the congregation of the saints, women should remain silent in the churches. They are not allowed to speak, but must be in submission, as the Law says. (I Cor. 14:34) (NIV)

The United Methodists: We affirm women and men to be equal in every aspect of their common life. We, therefore, urge that every effort be made to eliminate sex role stereotypes in activity and portrayal of family life . . . in the church and society . . . . We affirm the importance of women in decision-making positions at all levels of church life. . . .[7]

(Once again, their logic is in error. The fact that women are of equal worth does not at all imply that men and women must, or should, assume the same offices and roles. Indeed, the fact that they were created different should tell us otherwise).

Let the reader judge for himself whether or not an inconsistency exists here.

The tendency of some churches to ignore the Biblical teachings concerning such issues as homosexuality, adultery, and fornication, the role of women in the church, and the qualifications for positions of spiritual leadership in the church, have already been mentioned. Not only have some denominations considered ordaining homosexuals to the ministry, but one denomination has even devised a plan where by each church must have representatives on its board of elders for each sex, ethnic minority, and even for the young people.[8] Apparently, the Biblical commands that an elder be a man of strong spiritual stature have been discarded.

Just recently, a controversy was sizzling within the United Presbyterian Church (USA), as they have approved for ordination a man who denies the deity of Christ. After an appeal, the decision has been upheld by the denomination's Permanent Judicial Commission.[9]

How much worse can things get than this: a church which denies the deity of its own Savior? Are idol worship and temple prostitution also about to come back into vogue? We should not even consider these things beyond the realm of possibility. So long as Christians continue to go to these churches week after week and continue to give them their time, money, and support, there is no limit to what they might do.

Consider, for instance, the remarks one woman, ordained in the

United Presbyterian Church (USA), wrote in an article recently:

> I personally hate the pulpit and all it stands for. My theology emphasizes the Word made flesh, and not the Word enunciated in bell tones over the presumably sin-filled mobs below. Besides, my sisters down through history have been castigated from that pulpit. Not for nothing is the root of "scaffold" the same as "pulpit."
>
> I would rather take my hand mike and become a Sunday stroller into the crowd, touching and speaking directly to, hugging and ministering with all who seek nurture. I would raise my arms before the alter and praise my Creator in song and dance, timbrel and harp—making a joyful noise that speaks to the seasons of change and the profoundly earthly nature of our religious expression. I mean, who needs a "Mighty Fortress" except to hide behind?
>
> Now, whom shall we worship in this distinctly feminine ministry? I like Mary, Queen of Heaven, Moon Goddess, Mother of the Divine Son with whom she "mates" and causes to have an earthly death in the flesh and therefore a transcendence to eternal life.
>
> She is, of course, virgin—"one unto herself." She needs no male God figure to affirm and potentiate her powers . . . as the male religion emphasizes. . . .
>
> The Bible is full of allusions to tiny bright threads of goddess worship, and the contingent fear this caused the patriarchs. Jesus gathered 12 around Him—making 13—therefore not only a Covenant but a Coven as well.
>
> Get the linguistic picture? Like any good believer in the feminine principle and masculine principle in spiritual life, Jesus sees to it that the number is reinstated when Judas cops out on them. There can be no Coven(ant) without the 13. So He sends the Holy Spirit in His place after death.[10]

Those who have, until this point, had doubts concerning whether the churches could actually become worse than they presently are, leave them here.

How much more are we going to tolerate? How far must these men go before we will put a stop to this nonsense? Don't give your time, money, and support to a church which supports these kinds of things.

Perhaps the most encouraging point about our situation is that while many of the larger mainline churches are controlled by radical elements, most factors seem to indicate that the majority of laymen do not share their orientation. While the leadership of these denominations may not be truly Christian, or may in some cases even be attempting to advance Marxist or socialist philosophies in our culture, most surveys tend to show that the congregations are generally more conservative. Indeed, most of these denominations are currently losing members; this is clearly an indication that the church members are not content.

If it were possible to organize these various congregations apart from the leadership of such churches, it would probably not be too difficult for the churches, united, to remove these degenerate men, and place in their stead, men of strong Christian character. If this can be accomplished, so much the better; but in most cases this is at best a difficult task, if not impossible. Generally, the most practical step that an individual can take, in denominations such as these, is to leave, and perhaps take as many others with him as possible—even the whole congregation. Education is an important step here; we must do everything we can to keep others in the church, and the public in general, aware of what these churches are doing. This may be of benefit not only because it helps the Christian decide to which church he should go, but such negative publicity may even serve to shame these wayward churches back into orthodoxy.

But while we have no way of knowing whether God has ordained for a reformation to take place in this age or not, we can be sure of one thing: God is not in favor of a worldly church, a church which has goals other than His, and He will not allow it to remain in such a condition indefinitely. Whenever the church has fallen into a degenerate state, God has always reformed it by some means. On the rare occasions that the church became dominant in a society and turned currupt, God has brought about rebellions to overthrow the heirarchy. Or as is more commonly the case, the church becomes apathetic and stagnant, and God sends conquest, persecution, or whatever necessary to wake it up. We see this happening continually throughout the church's history; not only in the New Testament church, but in the Old as well. No matter how corrupt the church may become, God will always bring it back to Himself.

The real question before us, then, is not, "Will God reform the church of such corruption?" but rather, "How will He reform it—through self-cleansing now, or persecution later?" Reform always involves a return to submission to the authority of God, both by separating from the ungodly and by the further discipline of the true believers. But this can be achieved in more than one way, and if the church does not apply itself to these matters now, God can generate the same results in less pleasant ways. (Persecution does an especially fine job of driving out the unsaved and worldly elements, as well as forcing the Christian into a higher state of discipline.) Either we must strive to keep the church as pure and clear of sin as possible, or God will be forced to reform it in spite of us.

While it is true that God is sovereign over all these things, each Christian still has the responsibility of thinking on this matter, and will be held accountable for the decision he makes. He can either decide to go ahead and obey the Lord, and honestly strive for the purity and holiness of His church, or else he can continue to ignore the situation, and pay later. The Christian is not expected to make the church on earth perfect, of course; God does not expect the impossible from us. The church will only truly be perfect when He makes it perfect in the next world. But God does expect His followers to put Him first in their lives, and in the church as a whole. He wants a church which, while maybe not yet perfect, at least desires to be so; and one which honestly wants to exist solely for the purpose of knowing Him and doing His will. Perhaps the important thing to remember here is that whatever God wants, He will get; the means He will have to use to get it is up to us.

FOOTNOTES

Introduction
1. Charley Reese, "Church Group Supports African Terrorists," *The Journal Messenger*, (Manassas, VA), (Sept. 8, 1978), p.4.
2, 3. Editorial in *The Presbyterian Journal*, (Feb. 4, 1981), p.3.
3. The Presbyterian Church (US) spent $92,166.00 in the years 1971 and 1972 to obtain abortions for 341 people. One of the reasons for which this particular church endorsed abortions was the "socio-economic condition" of the family. The Steering Committee For A Continuing Presbyterian Church, *Which Way?—Abortion*, (Perry, Georgia), 1973.

Chapter 1
1. From *Calvin: Institutes of the Christian Religion*, edited by John T. McNeill, translated by Ford Lewis Battles, (Vol. XX, The Library of Christian Classics), copyright © MCMLX, W. L. Jenkins, used by permission of The Westminster Press; Book I, VII, 1, pp. 75.

Chapter 2
1. A more thorough account of these processes of regeneration and sanctification can be found in "The Reformed Doctrine of Predestination," by Loraine Boettner, available from The Presbyterian and Reformed Publishing Co.; Philadelphia, Pennsylvania, from which much of the material in this and preceding paragraphs was derived.

Chapter 3
1. Loraine Boettner, *"The Reformed Doctrine of Predestination,"* (Philadelphia, Pennsylvania; The Presbyterian and Reformed Publishing Company, 1977), p. 69, 70.

Chapter 4
1. Some manuscripts include the words "against you" at this point, which could possibly be interpreted to mean that our duty of confrontation is limited exclusively to those cases where the sin is committed against us personally. We can see, however, that this is not so, as there are numerous other passages which instruct us to counsel those who fall into sin under any circumstances (See Gal. 6:1, 2). Even if this one passage is taken in the stricter sense, the principles set forth still hold in the broader sense.

Chapter 7
1. Editorial comment in *The Presbyterian Journal*, (April 2, 1980), pp. 3.
    Charley Reese, "Church Group Supports African Terrorists," *The Journal Messenger*, (Manassas, VA), (Sept. 8, 1978), pp. 4.
2. Herman Nickel, "The Corporation Haters," *Fortune*, (June 16, 1980), pp. 126-136.
3. "Judicial Insanity (II)," *The Presbyterian Journal*, (Dec. 24, 1980), pp. 16-17.
4. From *The Book of Discipline of the United Methodist Church*, 1980. Copyright © 1980 by The United Methodist Publishing House, used by permission, pp. 78.
5. Ibid, pp. 89.
6. Ibid, pp. 101.
7. Ibid, pp. 93.
8. "Of 'Authentic' Churches," *The Presbyterian Journal*, (Nov. 26, 1980), pp. 10.
9. "An Apostate Church?" *The Presbyterian Journal*, (April 1, 1981), pp. 13.
    "UPCUSA Judicial Unit Upholds Kaseman," *The Presbyterian Journal*, (Feb. 11, 1981), pp. 6.
10. Joan Vassar-Williams, "From A Distinctly Feminine Clergywoman," *Monday Morning*, (March 23, 1981), pp. 9-12.